Things I Learned About My Dad
(in Therapy)

Things I Learned About My Dad (in Therapy)

essets

~~~~~~

Edited by
Heather B. Armstrong

𝓴

KENSINGTON BOOKS
www.kensingtonbooks.com

KENSINGTON BOOKS are published by

Kensington Publishing Corp.
850 Third Avenue
New York, NY 10022

All Kensington titles, imprints, and distributed lines are available at special quantity discounts for bulk purchases for sales promotion, premiums, fund-raising, educational or institutional use.

Special book excerpts or customized printings can also be created to fit specific needs. For details, write or phone the office of the Kensington Special Sales Manager: Kensington Publishing Corp., 850 Third Avenue, New York, NY 10022. Attn. Special Sales Department. Phone: 1-800-221-2647.

Kensington and the K logo Reg. U.S. Pat. & TM Off.

ISBN-13: 978-0-7582-1660-1
ISBN-10: 0-7582-1660-2

First Printing: May 2008
First Trade Paperback Printing: May 2009
10 9 8 7 6 5 4 3 2 1

Printed in the United States of America

This is for my dad, who is the reason the opera is in me.

Contents

Part Three: After the War

Introduction

When brainstorming ideas for this anthology, I thought it would be interesting to ask several of my fellow bloggers—some who are friends, others whose work I have admired online for years—to contribute their thoughts on fatherhood. As a woman and a mother, I am intrigued by the male perspective on parenthood, what it means to the man, and what it has meant to their children. My instructions were simple: I asked the writers to submit essays about fatherhood and left it up to them to decide whether they wanted to write about their husbands, their own fathers, or their own experiences as fathers. Initially, I expected this collection to be uproariously funny, as most of these writers are known to provide much-needed comic relief to their audiences. But as the essays came in, I was surprised to find a more layered narrative, and this book is filled with so much more than a series of physical pratfalls. Here you will find a love story rich with admiration, acceptance, recognition, and, finally, forgiveness. Yes, many of the essays are laugh-out-loud funny; some of them have to be, because humor is the only way to work through having to yell your child's name so many times that it transforms into a series of meaningless consonants echoing back and forth between the mounds of crap they have collected on the sofa. But many of them show that in the process of becoming a parent, we have had to confront everything we've ever wanted to ignore about our own fathers, how we have learned to accept who they were and who they are; and in doing so we can forgive ourselves a little bit.

I know that this exercise was therapeutic for many of the writers, myself included, and after I got everything down on paper I felt like had just had my brain dissected by a team of psychologists. Like any good therapy session, it made me move past the urge to blame my father for any impact his imperfections had on my life and instead recognize that I can only hope to do half as good a job as he did raising children, because God knows this isn't easy.

Part One

CONSCRIPTED

Ten Conclusions from Four
Years of Fatherhood

Kevin Guilfoile

The seventeen-year cicadas were coming in three days. The TV news was preparing us all for the onslaught. When the temperature of the soil reached a certain degree Fahrenheit, tens of millions of them would emerge at once from the ground, hundreds of thousands of them on every acre, and their giant bug bodies, big as thumbs, would fill the air like Beijing smog, madly mating in a public display of affection that would make Caligula want to reach for a towel. Their collective call would be louder than lawn mowers, so loud that for weeks you wouldn't be able to converse on the porch without shouting. Just stepping outside would be a harrowing affair, as cicadas, despite their enormous veined wings, fly much in the manner of William Katt on the old television show *The Greatest American Hero*—rudely off balance, hurtling through the air at high speed until they hit something, usually each other or the back of your head. Millions of moulted shells and rotting cicada corpses would litter the streets, crunching underfoot as you walked. And then there was the smell. Throughout the stifling wet heat of summer the neighborhood would smell like a massive un-air-conditioned insect morgue.

But that ordeal wouldn't begin for three more days. This particular afternoon was lovely and sunny and not too hot. It was still quiet. The sidewalks were clear. The air smelled like pollen and clean sheets. My three-year-old, Max—not a television news watcher—was oblivious to the impending swarm, and he and I were playing golf in the yard with oversized plastic clubs.

"I don't think I want to play outside anymore, Daddy," he said.

"Why not?" I asked.

Max's eyes followed a lone bee, some ten feet away, bouncing from red flower to yellow flower to purple one.

"Too many bugs," he said.

I thought, *There's so much he doesn't know.*

Max doesn't know that we're at war, or that countries even have wars. He doesn't know about Hail Mary passes or walk-off home runs. He doesn't know he's Irish. He doesn't know that Mom and Dad and the cat are going to die someday. He doesn't know why you put gas in the car or peas in your baby brother. He doesn't know about The Clash. He doesn't know we've been to the moon or why that was such a big deal. He doesn't know how soap works.

Although, now that I think about it, I'm not entirely clear how soap works either.

The things he does know are curiously arbitrary. He knows Chewbacca and R2-D2. He can spell *Mississippi.* He knows about Sufjan Stevens and John Hiatt and (perhaps inappropriately) Franz Ferdinand. He knows how to get dressed and un-dressed by himself, although he won't.

There has to be a correct order in which to learn all this stuff. A hierarchy of general knowledge. Maybe that's why so many people are homeschooling these days. Maybe they think they've figured out exactly how Jor-El used that talking crystal to explain the mysteries of the universe to Superman, and they're setting up their own Fortresses of Solitude at their dining room tables. Max, on the other hand, is learning everything the way I did—on a need-to-know basis. When he gets too close to the stove, I tell him that it's hot. When he gets too close to the cat, I tell him to be gentle. And it's probably better for the child, I rationalize, that he follows his curiosity and figures it all out on his own. As his dad, I am sort of his Wikipedia—a massive repository of sometimes deliberately falsified information that he can call upon, but only when needed.

In fact, my own, probably faulty, recollection of childhood was that my parents would truthfully discuss any and all un-comfortable topics with me, but only if I asked a specific ques-tion. And like a reluctant witness on the stand, they would only answer yes or no. Which led to conversations like this:

ME: Do girls have penises?
THEM: No.

And then I would spend the next several weeks formulating a new theory and carefully crafting my follow-up.

They say kids are sponges and that they'll learn at an astonishing pace, and I suppose that's true. But fatherhood has a pretty steep learning curve as well, and there are at least ten things I know now that I didn't know before I was a dad. Of course, the genre of writing known as "The things we learn from the kids we're supposed to be teaching" is too often the source of awful, sentimental prose. Sadly, we parents can't help ourselves, which is why . . .

1. Before I had kids of my own, I found parents really annoying.

When you have a child, the whole point of it becomes pretty clear pretty rapidly. Babies come into the world as completely selfish organisms, incapable of thinking about anything but their own desires. Over the next twenty years or so it's the parents' job to make them a little more self-sufficient and just a little bit less selfish. That's it really. That's all parenting is.

But the crazy thing the universe does is that it frequently gives kids to us after anywhere between five and fifteen glorious adult years of being single and free. And after five or fifteen years of pursuing grown-up pleasures with the same gusto that infants pursue milk and pants-crapping and shoving into their mouths household detritus exactly the diameter of their esophagi, you realize you and the baby are pretty much exactly the same, except all the responsibility falls on you, and in giving up everything to make this baby a little less selfish, you find you've made yourself a little less selfish as well.

Except nobody wants to hear about that crap, so keep it to yourself.

2. Don't ask your doctor for the sex of your baby.

Before he's born, I mean. Afterward you should definitely ask or you risk really screwing the kid up. But when he's still womb-bound, you should keep it all mysterious, partly because it's fun to be surprised and partly because you'll want to have something interesting to announce besides the baby's length and weight. Length is a totally arbitrary statistic to be putting on a birth announcement, but other than penis/vagina, it's just about the only quantifiable thing we can say about a baby at that point. You could print the circumference of his or her skull and it would be exactly as meaningful. If God were funnier, all your baby's physical traits would be as random as the sex. Then sisters and parents of the new mom would be in charge of putting a giant wooden stork in your front yard announcing, IT'S AN ASIAN!

3. Don't sweat too much over your baby's name.

Pick something you like, of course. Pick something you won't get tired of saying fourteen times in a row. ("Kevin. Kevin. Kevin. Kevin. Kevin! Kevin, come here. *Kevin!* Kevin. Come. Here. Kevin! Right now! I said *come here!* KEVIN!! KEVIN!!!! *KEVIN!!!!!!!!!!!*) But know this: If you have a boy, no matter the name you give him, Tard is what he will eventually be called. Tard is every American boy's name at some point. It's just a question of how many degrees of separation from Tard you are. For me it went like this: "Kevin, Caveman, Neanderthal, Australopithecus, Astroturf, Astrotard, Tard." There's no getting around it, so you might as well not worry and name your kid Tad from the get-go. At least it will be quick.

> *Before I had a child, I thought parents were comically*
> *poop-obsessed, but now I totally get it.*

4. You will become obsessed with feces.

Before I had a child, I thought parents were comically poop-obsessed, but now I totally get it. When you have an infant, a healthy poop is the equivalent of a hearty "All's well!" from the town crier. Poop is the closest thing a baby has to language. It tells you if they're feeling bad and exactly where it hurts. But it also gets everywhere and on everything, including you, and you learn to just shrug and wipe it all off with a wet napkin. You become completely inured to the sights and smells and texture of steaming hot crap. In fact, just take it for granted that for the next three years your house is going to smell like a Bolivian prison.

Of course, during this time your child overcomes his own God-given disgust of his own waste, as well, and eventually he won't mind sitting in it for hours on end when he should be learning to use the toilet. If you had told me three years ago that the hardest part of being a parent would be convincing my child that thousands of years of civil engineering have produced ever more sophisticated means of removing waste product from the home and he doesn't have to walk around with his pants full of ripe feces, I would have called you insane.

On the other hand, maybe I should find another way to explain it to him.

5. *There is no miracle diaper disposal machine that can transcend the immutable laws of physics.*

At some point during the baby-shower registration process, you and your partner, otherwise intelligent and rational people, will become convinced that there are magical products into which you deposit a stinky diaper and deliver it to another dimension. *Diaper Champ. Diaper Genie. Diaper Wormhole.* Whatever the evil sales copy says, understand these are nothing more than cheap plastic cans with snap-on lids. For several nights in a row, while rocking the boy to sleep, you will sniff a pungent odor, and when you go to change him, you will realize the odor is not coming from your child but rather from the gigantic bucket of three-day-old shit sitting four feet away from your face. Even zoo monkeys are smart enough to hurl their fresh feces to the other side of the cage, but somehow new parents think their child's poop will keep just fine until garbage day in a porous bucket next to his crib. Honestly, your college degree is worthless.

6. *You will become a hypochondriac by proxy.*

It will start when you become obsessed with every burp and gurgle (and poop) your baby makes and it will worsen exponentially when you begin to worry about developmental benchmarks. Reading parenting books will only make it worse. You will be more familiar with the symptoms of childhood disease and abnormality than a pediatric resident. CF? MS? CP? SB? Pyloric stenosis? Intestinal atresia? Hirschsprung's disease? Turner's syndrome? Sickle cell? Clubfoot? Dysplasia? Deformational plagiocephaly? Tetralogy of Fallot? Pulmonary stenosis? He could have any of that! All of it! Call the doctor now!

When you do call the doctor, you will usually get a nurse, who has been required to take and pass a special training course in which she learns not to laugh audibly over the phone at hysterical parents whose kid has just crawled over a LEGO.

When my son was four months old, he developed a bright red rash that started at the top of his head and began moving down his body like a flame on an oil-soaked rope. I rushed him to the doctor, who walked in the exam room and said, "What's the problem?" I said, "My son has a rash!" He put on his glasses and said, "Yep." Three hundred dollars.

7. Your home will be a total disaster for the foreseeable future.

When I was a kid, my mother raised four kids and kept an immaculate house. I'm a stay-at-home dad and try to pick up, but now that I'm home all day, my net contribution to household cleanliness is apparently negative. For the first time in our marriage we've had to hire a cleaning lady, not so much to clean up after the kids but to clean up after *me*. Actually, I'm happy to do my part, but apparently as a man, my understanding of "clean" is materially different from my wife's. And there's really nothing you can do about the smell (see Number 4).

8. *If your first child is a good baby, quit having them.*

No one ever says, "My first baby was an angel, and the second one was even better!" If the first one is easygoing and healthy, the universe will punish you for it. Your second child will almost certainly grow up to be a stripper/cannibal who invents airborne cancer and kills off his babysitters one at a time with a Big Wheel.

9. *Try to talk about something else instead of your kids all the time.*

Talking constantly about your kids completely undermines your primary mission of making them less self-absorbed. As I mentioned at the outset, nobody likes to hear you go on and on and on about them. So just assume that everyone knows your kids are great and that you love them to pieces and talk about something else every once in a while. Sports. Popular music. The hue and texture of your lawn.

Or politics. For instance, one of the things I've noticed is that being the parent of a toddler is a lot like being the most powerful nation in the world trying to control an occupied foreign land. On the face of it, it seems like we have all the power and should be able to tame this child and mold him in our image. To dictate his constitution, as it were. But there's the language problem. And even when both of us are home, there aren't enough boots on the ground. He gets most of his information from a kids' version of Al Jazeera known as the Disney Channel. Plus, the little insurgent has learned very quickly that there are certain lines we just won't cross and so he's pretty much not afraid of us. He knows that he can scream longer and louder than the folks back home will tolerate. And he takes an unreasonable all-or-nothing stance when it comes to negotiations: If the insurgent wants a banana, a perfectly logical explanation for why he cannot have one, like "Those bananas aren't ripe," is insufficient. He sees bananas and demands that the corrupt interim government distribute them at once.

10. *They will be older than you were at that age.*

It was ninety degrees and the heat made the cicadas even more amorous than usual, and their swarming and bumping and shrieking made playing outside almost impossible. Max's friend Bella, also three, was over to the house and they were on the couch watching television.

"Are you cold, Bella? I'm cold," Max said. "I'm going to get under this blanket. Would you like to get under this blanket with me?"

She did, and giggling to myself, I took a picture of them. They were so cute.

Three days later another three-year-old girl from the neighborhood, Norah, was over to play. She picked up the photograph of Max and Bella cuddling under a blanket. She studied it a moment and then flipped it over so I could see it and pointed an accusing finger my way.

"Um," she said, her voice spiked with jealousy, "where was *I*?"

Shoot, *that* didn't happen to me until I was twenty-three.

༄

Kevin Guilfoile's debut novel, Cast of Shadows, *was published in 2005 by Alfred A. Knopf and has been translated into more than fifteen languages. He is a regular contributor to themorningnews.org, coudal.com, and theoutfitcollective.com. He lives in La Grange, Illinois, with his wife and sons.*

Sam I Am

Matthew Baldwin

When my wife was eight months pregnant, she and I went to see *The Return of the King*. We had no other children and no prior experience in child-rearing, but some instinct warned us that we ought to make one last trip to the cinema while able, before our entertainment options were abruptly reduced to scrubbing applesauce off the walls, reading 27-word books about anthropomorphic mice, and after putting the tyke to bed, slumping off to sleep 10 minutes into a DVD.

The Return of the King is, of course, the third and final film in the *Lord of the Rings* trilogy, a series I had read twice and was now enjoying immensely on the silver screen. And yet, until that viewing, I never grokked the central symbolism of the story. On this particular occasion, though, I was struck by an epiphany about halfway through the film.

"Hey, wait a minute," I muttered to myself, handful of popcorn arrested on its journey to my mouth. "I know what this is about. This whole saga is an allegory for pregnancy!"

It seems so obvious in retrospect. The story, you may recall, centers around Frodo, Sam, and their quest to deliver the One Ring to the Crack of Doom. Much of the third film documents their slow and laborious trudge to Mordor. That's the first tip-off, right there. Has there ever been a more appropriate euphemism for pregnancy than "trudging to Mordor"?

> *Has there ever been a more appropriate euphemism*
> *for pregnancy than "trudging to Mordor"?*

In *The Lord of the Rings,* as in life, only one person is the appointed bearer, obliged to carry the load the entire way. A burden that gets heavier and heavier as the weeks wear on, and one that makes the bearer increasingly tired and cranky.

And the bearer's companion, be he husband or Halfling? What does he do? Not much, honestly, except occasionally administer foot rubs and/or fight off enormous spiders. The rest of the time he just trails along, as useful as the white crayon in a Crayola 8-pack, doing what he can to keep morale high and lamenting the fact that he can't carry the burden once in a while.

But as bad as the journey is, the final moments are much, much worse. Having arrived at their destination, be it delivery room or active volcano, it's suddenly discovered that releasing the burden is even more difficult than carrying it. "I can't do it," the bearer cries, "it's impossible!" The companion does what little he can, offering words of encouragement, but the bearer turns on him in snarling fury.

And then the journey abruptly ends, as a creepy-looking bald-headed creature comes on to the scene.

The analogy seems pretty straightforward to me, though,

admittedly, I haven't worked out all the parallels. For instance, in *The Lord of the Rings* there is an unstoppable, malevolent force that can't wait to get its hands on the thing the bearer is carrying. I'm not sure what this corresponds to in real life. I'm going to guess McDonald's.

∽

When my wife and I decided to give pregnancy a whirl, I had this idea that the enterprise would be like carrying a couch. I would grab one end, she would grab the other, and together we would share the load.

Come to learn, an unborn child is less like a couch and more like a box of books: very heavy, but too small to be ported by more than one person. Essentially you wind up with one person doing all the work while the other "supervises," or just runs ahead, opening doors and shooing the cat out of the path.

This is problematic for self-anointed progressive males such as myself, who have been taught to "share the load" on any project they undertake with their partner. One person makes the dinner, the other does the dishes—that kind of thing. But only in a family where the man routinely makes dinner in two minutes and somehow generates a quantity of dishes that requires nine months to clean can pregnancy be considered even remotely comparable.

Some fathers try to disguise this fact with first-person plurals. As in, "Great news: we're pregnant!" I could never bring myself to adopt this phrase, chiefly because it is dumb. Let's be honest: the only time the word "we" should be paired with "pregnant" is when the speaker is royalty or a conjoined twin.

It's one of those rare circumstances where blatant lying isn't the solution, but I freely admit that it's a tough situation. You partner spends nearly a year bringing new life into the world, and you're the guy getting paid $13 an hour to stand around holding a WOMAN AT WORK sign for passing motorists.

∽

This asymmetry begins even before conception, when the woman is expected to get her womb in order, like a family hastily tidying up a home in anticipation of guests.

To aid in this endeavor, prepregnancy books provide an exhaustive list of tasks for the mama-to-be. And then, at the very end, tack on a sentence or so of paternal prerequisites.

Prospective Mother

- Get a complete battery of physicals.
- Stop consuming alcohol.
- Stop consuming caffeine.
- Stop smoking.
- Eat a well-balanced diet.
- Take vitamins.
- Exercise more.
- Reduce stress.

Prospective Father

- Keep testicles away from radiation and machinery with moving parts.

So while my wife had to change pretty much every aspect of her waking life, all I had to do was stop operating my steam-powered printing press in the nude. Perhaps a disappointment for the sixty-seven subscribers to *Ceramic Dixie* (my monthly zine featuring photographs of key Civil War battles recreated with Hummel figurines), but really not much of a hardship for me. Sperm are apparently so cheap and plentiful that doing anything to protect them is like taking out an insurance policy on a tube sock.

Needless to say, my wife was a little bitter about the inequity of preparation. She had to swear off coffee and red wine and cheeseburgers. She had to visit the doctor and the gym. She had to take prenatal vitamin supplements containing more minerals than the Museum of Geological History. Meanwhile, my performance, in terms of conception, was going to be graded pretty much entirely on attendance.

Actually, there was one other thing the books asked men to do before baby-making: stop using illicit drugs. Unfortunately this didn't apply to me, as I'd lacked the foresight to get hooked on any before the blessed event.

So whenever my friends tell me that they are thinking about having a child, I will take the prospective dad aside at some point and urge him to start using heroin immediately. "Kicking the habit will be rough," I warn him, "what with the agonizing detox and crippling withdrawal symptoms. But it's either that or don't give up anything before conception, and endure nine months of your wife's withering resentment. So it's pretty much a no-brainer."

∾

The diet regimen for pregnant women is, if anything, even more draconian than for those merely contemplating motherhood. The truth is that there is an entire industry of books in the "What to Expect" mold, which characterize the human womb as the most precarious location on Earth, one that will instantly implode if exposed to anything other than organically grown leafy green vegetables, harvested by naiads by the light of the moon.

We learned this from a book called *Every Woman's Guide to Eating During Pregnancy,* chock full of the kind of dishes that make a vegan giddy. Every recipe was structured around some food you normally wouldn't eat unless lost in a forest. Typically 14 of the 16 ingredients were spices (¼ teaspoon nutmeg, ⅛ teaspoon cumin) to disguise the fact that you were essentially eating two pounds of chard.

(Funny aside: Around the commencement of Pregnancy, Act III, I was talking to a colleague, and mentioned that my wife had just entered the third trimester. "Ah yes," said my coworker, "she's entering the salad days." "Holy crap," was my terrified response. "We're going to be eating even *more* salad?!")

So at least I was able to help in the preparation of, and suffering through, these meals. Stoically chocking down Arugula Surprise ("Surprise! You've been reduced to eating arugula!") assuaged my guilt somewhat. I was proud to be providing misery plenty of the company it is reputed to love.

Of course, my wife knew where my real skills lay: to rouse myself from the couch at 11:00 P.M., several hours after our 37-calorie dinner, and at her command, fetch chocolate ice cream and corn dogs from the local grocery store.

∽

The other contribution I made to the pregnancy was accompanying my wife to childbirth classes. As we live in progressive Seattle, nearly all the women in attendance were accompanied by the fathers, even though we really didn't do much beyond gawp in horror at the delivery videos and exclaim, "Holy smokes! That's going to totally suck for you, honey."

The sessions covered the nuts and bolts of labor: breathing techniques, coping mechanisms, and what to say when your child comes out. ("That doesn't look like a baby!" was a popular exclamation in the films we saw.) Most of this was intended for the mothers, obviously, but we did cover a few dad-centric topics, like how to take a punch while your wife is in the "transition stage."

We also learned that the father of the child traditionally cuts the umbilical cord. "Why?" I asked. Our teacher seemed confused by the question, so I clarified. "I mean, is there an actual reason for the father to do it, because he's standing right there anyhow and the midwife's hands are full? Or is this just to make the husband feel useful? So, later, with the guys, he can be all, like, 'Oh dude, I *totally* helped deliver that baby!'?"

The teacher conceded that the latter was the case.

Knowing that the cord cutting is purely ceremonial, I resolved to go whole hog. I told my wife I was going to wear a suit with a sash reading DAD, and would proclaim, "I declare this baby to be . . . born!" while cutting the cord with a giant pair of novelty scissors. This plan was inexplicably vetoed.

∾

Finally, the big day arrived at last. Here is the exhaustive list of things I did from the moment my wife went into labor to when I officially became a father.

Timed Contractions

"That baby better hurry, if he wants to get born on time." So joked I, around 10 P.M. on my wife's due date.

Ninety minutes later I stood, stopwatch in hand, marking off seconds between contractions. "It *heard* you!" my wife said. "I could be *sleeping* right now. But noooo, you had to go and induce labor!"

In birthing class they told us not to go to the delivery room until the contractions had fallen into a predictable rhythm for at least an hour, thus avoiding the possibility of false alarm. We called the hospital after 40 minutes and told them that my wife's contractions were so consistent that I, the guy with the stopwatch, was telling *her* when they were going to occur. ("Three . . . two . . . one . . . aaaand agony.")

"Jeez, really?" the lady on the other end said. "Get over here immediately."

Drove to the Hospital at Approximately Eight Miles an Hour

In movies, the flustered husband loads his wife into the vehicle and drives to the emergency room at the speed of sound, weaving in and out of traffic and shouting breathing instructions over his shoulder as he blows through stoplights and careens into hot dog vendors.

We puttered. Lollygagged, even. Seattle is beautiful at night, and we took in the scenery, moseying along at 5 mph below the speed limit so as not to attract the attention of the authorities. We even chatted amicably about the situation, albeit in four-minute segments. My wife spent every fifth minute with her back arched, clutching the door handle and screaming, "Oh my God FLOOR IT!" But 60 seconds later we'd again be making chitchat, politely disagreeing about whether "meat loaf" was one word or two.

Set the Mood

Upon our arrival, my wife was given a quick examination, and told that the baby already had his little hobo bindle over his shoulder, ready to jump train at the next depot.

Like Batman to the scene of a crime, I leapt into action. Extracting an iPod and set of speakers from our backpack, I rushed into the delivery room to set up an ad hoc stereo system.

One of our many pregnancy books mentioned music during labor, offhandedly suggesting that familiar and comfortable songs might aid in relaxation and make the entire process a smidge more bearable. Seizing upon this as Something I Could Do, I spent weeks creating and rejiggering playlists, trying to establish the perfect atmosphere for having a small person come out of your private parts. "Oh yeah," I'd say to myself, sitting at my PC, rearranging songs for the umpteenth time. "Nelly Furtado is *perfect* nine-centimeters-dilated music."

Even to this day we'll talk about this. When a Suzanne Vega song comes on the radio, I'll say, "Hey, this is what was playing when our son was born!" And my wife replies, "There was music in the delivery room?"

Frantically Tried to Keep Up with "Cannonball" Baldwin

Once I hit "play" on the iPod, I became largely superfluous.

There was a host of things I was hypothetically responsible for, but the kid seemed determined to thwart me at every turn. For example, it was my solemn duty to ensure that my wife received a panoply of Fantastic Drugs. But by the time we arrived at the hospital, the issue was academic—the whole point of an epidural is to get the mother through "transition," a stage my wife had completed during the car ride. I asked if we could get the drugs in a doggie bag to go, but apparently that is frowned upon.

Instead, I concentrated on coaching my wife through the miracle of childbirth, calling upon the techniques we'd learned in class. But it quickly degenerated into a race between me and

my progeny. I'd say, "Okay, take short, distracting breaths to—"
and my wife would say, "Too late; I think it's coming," and I'd
say, "What, already?! Okay, well then you should—" and the
doctor would say, "Too late; here's the head!" and the next
thing I knew I was screaming "PUUUUUUUSH!" while
cutting the umbilical cord.

All told, my wife was in the delivery room for a little over
an hour. I can only assume that when the child heard my awesome mix of music through the uterine walls, he was eager to
enter a world where people with my caliber of iPod playlist-
making skills reside. So, see? I totally helped.

And so ended my Era of Uselessness.

Division of parenting duties gets immeasurably easier once
the baby is no longer embedded in one of the caregivers. Yes,
breastfeeding still falls entirely within the mother's bailiwick,
but a newborn generates plenty of work for a father to do as
well. We quickly adopted a system that was as efficient as it
was simple: Mama was in charge of what went into the baby;
Papa was in charge of what came out of the baby.

As time went on and our son grew older, we soon began to
adopt specific roles. All inquiries regarding roughhousing,
wrasslin', and horseplay are routinely directed to my department, for instance. And I also became the bedtime song-singer.
Nature blessed my wife with the ability to carry a child, but
alas, not a tune.

We've decided to stop at one child. Frankly, another pregnancy would just be too taxing. For me, I mean. Nine more
months of guilt? No thanks.

∾

Yesterday my son (now three) and I were monkeying around in the backyard. My wife strolled out to see what we were doing, and noticed that he was lugging around an object he had purloined from our small stash of building supplies. Curious, she turned to me for explanation.

WIFE: What is he carrying?
ME: It's a brick.
WIFE: He's walking around carrying a brick?
ME: That's correct.
{Pause}
WIFE: What if he drops it on his foot?
ME: Then he will learn not to drop bricks on his foot.

Conversations like this reassure me that the father has an important role in the child-rearing process. If you know not to drop a brick on your foot, thank a dad.

∾

A programmer by trade, Matthew Baldwin also writes the blog defective yeti, maintains the site tradetricks.org, is a contributing writer for themorningnews.org, and freelances for a number of publications. He lives in Seattle with his wife, his son, and some good-for-nothing cats.

A Girl Named Spike (And Other Gambles of a Godless Fatherhood)

Matthew D. LaPlante

Dear Spike:

Some of us enter this world kicking and screaming. You arrived perfectly silent. Your heart wasn't beating. Your lungs weren't breathing. You weren't moving.

As they rushed your tiny, gray body out of the delivery room, one of the nurses looked over her shoulder and told me to follow.

"Dad—come," was all that she said.

That was the first time anyone had called me by that name. It scared me. It still does.

Of all the names we have for God, the one we use most frequently is "Father." I imagine that says something about how our species sees God—as a bringer of life, protector, provider, and friend. But I worry it might also say something about how we see fathers. And I am not certain I am in favor of setting the bar that high.

I only briefly looked back at your mother. They'd ripped into her body to get you out and she was lying on the delivery table like a ravaged rag doll. The epidural had numbed her body, but of course it could not numb her fears. Her face was white, shocked. Her eyes were big and frightened. She had expected to hear your cries and to hold your wet, shivering body next to hers. Instead, she watched as they raced you away, unable to lift herself to follow. I can't imagine her fear and confusion at that moment. I wanted to go to her. I wanted to comfort her. But I ran after the nurse as instructed. That was my first act of fatherhood.

I could not have been less Godlike, chasing the doctors and nurses down a long white hall. I was scared and bewildered and thunderstruck—and helpless. In fact, of all the emotions that bolted through me in those moments, the most overwhelming was helplessness.

I could not bring you life. You were all of four pounds and I could not protect you. Those responsibilities fell to others. And so my first duty, as a father, was simply to follow you to the newborn intensive care unit—presumably so that no one would accidentally mix you up with some other four-pound, nearly stillborn child.

I didn't breathe. I didn't blink. I didn't swallow. I didn't dare speak. I simply watched. That was my job as someone else played God, recovering your heartbeat and bringing you breath when you had none.

Finally, blessedly finally, you cried. And when you did, I did too. Overjoyed. Relieved. Proud. And yet still very helpless. Far from Godlike. Far even from fatherlike.

I've had some time now to get used to being a father—or, at least, to get used to the idea of being a father. But I'm no closer to doffing that same oppressive helplessness I felt in those fearful first moments of your life. And I'm worried that I never will be—that I will somehow always be chasing after you, simply spectating.

Not that I'm likely to be let off that easy. Not that any father is.

I've been coaching soccer since I was a teenager. My mother is an elementary school teacher. So is your mother, as it happens. None of that makes me an expert on raising kids, but I've been around enough children, and their parents, to have noticed that fathers—even those who simply *act* as spectators to their children's lives—aren't ever simply spectators. There is, in fact, a conspicuous pattern of paternity. Good kids have good dads, bad kids have bad dads. And so it goes and goes.

There are exceptions, of course—children who somehow manage to rise above or fall below the quality of their rearing and the caliber of their genetic code. So I suppose there's hope for you, even if I mess things up.

And that's a distinct possibility. After all, you've already got plenty working against you. The genes I've passed your way include asthma, cancer, heart disease, diabetes, alcoholism, depression, and mental illness. Oh yeah, and bad teenage acne. I'm terribly sorry about that.

I can't change any of those things. Nature is as she is.

She gave you my ears and my lips. She gave you your mother's eyes and her chin. All things considered, you haven't done badly. People say you're beautiful. (They say that about all babies, of course, but they mean it when they say it about you.)

Perhaps you'll take from us a few other traits. Some good, I hope. Some bad, no doubt.

But which ones? I wish I could say. There are tens of thousands of books on the subject of parenting, although as far as I can tell, a definitive answer to the ancient question of nature versus nurture remains elusive. I've long believed, though, that we are more than crude models of our ancestors. We are more than our genetic code. Our personalities, our bodies, and even our souls are inextricably shaped by our experiences—and not only those experiences our parents plan for us or wish for us.

When I was very young, my father took me to the park so that we could test-fly the Batman kite I'd received as a present for my birthday. "There's really not much to it," he told me. "You'll get it up in the air and then the wind will take it from there—after that, you'll simply guide it."

He placed the roll of string in my hands and carried the kite out 10 or 15 yards. As he lifted it above his head, the outstretched string was pulled taut.

"Oh yeah," he said as Batman's cape began to flap in the breeze, "give it the best running start you can."

And with that, he let go.

When you're flying a kite, you simply run into the wind. But the wind blows differently for all of us, and prone to change directions at any moment, it is difficult to predict. So everyone's running start looks a bit different. For better or for worse, though, most fathers simply look down at the paths already cut by their own fathers and then run like mad. I suppose that's why good kids have good dads, bad kids have bad dads, and so it goes and goes.

But, of course, the wind takes it from there. And as it does, things become rather unpredictable.

So I am the father my father was. I am the father he taught

me to be. But I am also the father I learned to be, exclusive of him.

You, in turn, will be the person I am. You will be the person I will teach you to be. And you will be the person you learn to be, exclusive of me. So it goes and goes.

I suppose that leaves me standing somewhere between spectator and God—a good deal closer to spectator than God, I guess—but I think I am growing comfortable with that. I never wanted to hold all of your strings anyway. I only ever expected to be given just the one.

My father raised his children to fear him, but I never questioned his devotion or love for me. He spent long hours at work and long weeks on the road, and yet it never seemed as though he was not there. He was at once somber and affectionate, harsh and adoring. I hope you'll see some of those traits in me, as you grow, but I'm determined that you won't see them all. I imagine you'll make a similar resolution with your own children one day.

My mother always called me by my Christian name. My father always called me "Scooter"—even when he was angry. He'd always wanted a kid named Scooter. I'm not certain he even knew why. When I was growing up, he often coached my soccer and baseball teams. I don't think he called me by my given name once. And so neither did anyone else.

I suppose it could have been worse, though. He could have always wanted a kid named Muffin. Or Poopers.

In the grand psychological scheme of things, "Scooter" did me no harm. And I'm pretty sure I would have survived "Poopers," too. Hell, that might have distracted my teammates from a litany of more obvious things to make fun of—like my inability to kick or throw, for starters.

I tell you this by means of explaining, and perhaps excusing, the fact that while most fathers dote upon their daughters with names like "princess," "angel," "sweetheart," and "pumpkin," I call you "Spike."

I'm not a cruel person. Or white trash. For all it has since come to mean to me, your name started as a matter of convenience. It wasn't even my idea, really. Your mother and I were simply having a bit of trouble with pronouns.

Pronouns suck, by the way. You can tell your teacher that, if you'd like, someday. Just look her in the eye and say, "Pronouns suck, ma'am. My father told me so."

You see, in all its infinite glory, the English language is woefully inadequate. For one thing, there's no word to describe the feeling you get in your stomach when you wash down a jar of pickles with a half-gallon of chocolate milk. (Your grandmother will tell you this sensation is called "currywibbles," but I've yet to find that word in any dictionary.)

> *In all its infinite glory, the English language is woefully inadequate. For one thing, there's no word to describe the feeling you get in your stomach when you wash down a jar of pickles with a half-gallon of chocolate milk.*

An only slightly more egregious oversight is the lack of pronouns to describe someone whose gender is ambiguous, unimportant, or unknown. That can be annoying. And it can be amusing.

There's an old series of *Saturday Night Live* sketches about a person named Pat. Which began with a little ditty that went something like this:

> *A lot of people say, "What's that?" It's Pat!*
> *A lot of people ask, "Who's he? Or she?"*
> *A ma'am or a sir? Accept him or her—or whatever it may be.*

In the immediate days after learning your mother was pregnant, we used our pronouns interchangeably. I was inclined to say "he" and "him" and "his." Your mom more frequently used "she" and "her" and "hers." Neither of us felt comfortable calling you "it."

Your mother—she's never been comfortable with uncertainty—tired of our dueling pronouns within a few days.

"I think we should give our baby a temporary name," she suggested.

"Like Pat?" I asked.

She crinkled her nose.

"No," she said. "I think we should call it Spike."

So you see, it all began innocently enough: She'd been thinking about getting a dog and instead she got pregnant. "But there's no use wasting a perfectly good name," she explained.

Not everyone was amused—especially after we learned you were a girl. We adjusted our pronouns accordingly, of course, but by that time we'd grown too fond of Spike to call you anything else. Still, family members begged us to reconsider—or at least to contemplate "Spikette" as an alternative. Friends wondered if we weren't asking for trouble by choosing a name that invoked such a spirit of rebellion.

"She's going to make you pay for that name," a good friend told me as we were walking back to work from lunch one day.

"I imagine so," I told him.

"I mean one way or another," he continued. "I know what you're trying to do, and it's going to backfire. Forget Transformers and Ninja Turtles, man, she's gonna want Easy-Bake Ovens and Barbie dolls."

The protests weren't limited to people we knew. When your mother was about six months along, we were visiting the public library when—as pregnant women are wont to do—she made a mad dash for the restroom, rushing in as another woman was coming out.

The woman stepped aside to let your mother pass, then spotted me waiting by the drinking fountains.

"Was that your wife?" she asked.

I nodded my head.

"Looks like someone's going to have a baby," she said. Her manner was so sticky-sweet you'd think she'd arranged the whole thing herself.

She was one of those sadly conspicuous, middle-aged Mormon closet lesbians, so common in our fair city, who for reasons of either devout piety or deep self-loathing, wind up spending a lifetime like Eleanor Rigby, living vicariously through the mundane lives of others rather than succumbing to the sinful charms of another woman.

Maybe I'm just a grump, but I was already annoyed. I don't often care to speak about my family with strangers . . .

"No, actually she's just fat," I replied.

"Uh-huh, and when's the due date?"

Was she deaf to my sarcasm? Or just not listening? I tried again.

"As soon as I can find a coat hanger."

"Soon, then? Great! And what are you having?"

This situation obviously called for some bigger guns.

"Well, I was hoping for a hermaphrodite because there's a burgeoning porn market for those things—especially the young ones—but we're stuck with a girl."

"A girl! Oh, how sweet. A little angel! A tiny princess! She's going to have you wrapped around her little finger. Do you have a name picked out?"

My repartee was falling like a French army. I surrendered in kind.

"Yes, ma'am. We're calling her Spike."

"*Spike?*" she asked.

Surely this wasn't the moment she was going to begin paying attention.

"Right. Spike," I said.

"*Spike? Oh no, you're not going to do that. You just can't do that! Please tell me you're just joking . . .*

Well, *Vive le Sarcasme,* it turns out all it took was the truth. So, to recap: Say you're about to abort your own child with a dirty piece of scrap metal? That's not worthy of so much as a batted eyelash. But threaten to name a girl Spike? Call in the child protection caseworkers!

But who knows? Maybe she knew something I don't. Maybe I've condemned you to a life of crime. Of leather and tattoos and piercings and random other body alterations that no one has yet been debased enough to conceive. It's not out of the realm of possible consequences. For truly, could there be anything more elemental to who we become than what we are called?

Growing up, your mother knew two boys—identical twins from a Greek Orthodox family in her neighborhood—named Christian and Damien. As small wonders go, Christian grew up to be the more compassionate and caring of the two. Damien was the selfish and less social one.

Oh, to be a fly on the wall of that family's group therapy session! Were the boys simply living up to their names? Were they acting upon the shrouded expectations of others about who they should become? Or did some anomaly in their genetic code—identical though it should have been—bequeath to Christian a natural gentleness and to Damien an innate penchant for misbehavior?

So I suppose it is possible that I am gambling with your stars. But then, I am a betting man. And at the moment, I'm betting that what we've chosen to call you is just a starting place—perhaps slightly more consequential than Scooter and slightly less consequential than Poopers—a simple and perhaps not-so-subtle middle finger to a Disney princess culture that has made every little girl in America want to be Ariel, Sleeping Beauty, or Cinderella.

We own all those movies. I have no problem with those characters, I just don't want them to be your character. I'd rather you be . . . well . . . a Spike—worthy of every definition of the word. Sharp and strong. An abrupt rise over normalcy. Added flavor and intoxication to the punch of life.

∾

Sure, I'm raising you to raise hell. To ask questions and take risks and challenge convention. And as of rebellion? Of leather and tattoos and strange body piercings? Of Easy-Bake Ovens and Barbie dolls? Somewhere between the wishful thinking of a father who wants to play God with his daughter and the worried thinking of a father who understands his unequalness to that task is a rather simple reality: There will be some things I can control and there will be some things I cannot.

> *Somewhere between the wishful thinking of a father who wants to play God with his daughter and the worried thinking of a father who understands his unequalness to that task is a rather simple reality: There will be some things I can control and there will be some things I cannot.*

You taught me that lesson before you even gasped your first breath. Certainly, those moments left me humbled and feeling helpless as a father in ways that have not faded in the months that have followed. And I do not expect them to.

But maybe I can give you a running start in just the right direction. To catch the wind in just the right way. To lift you off the ground.

I'm a betting man, but not even I would wager on where the wind will take you from there. But wherever you go, Spike, whatever you do and whatever you become, you will be loved.

Unconditionally. And forever.

Love,

Dad

∽

Matthew D. LaPlante is a father, husband, soccer fanatic, wine maker, poker player, motorcyclist, painter, blogger, journalist, and author. As national security reporter for The Salt Lake Tribune, LaPlante has covered military operations from Iraq, Kuwait, Turkey, Germany, and throughout the United States, in addition to feature reporting assignments in Israel, the West Bank, Spain, and Ecuador. A veteran of the U.S. Navy, in which he served as an intelligence analyst, LaPlante holds a bachelor's degree in politics and the media from Oregon State University. A native of California, he currently resides in Salt Lake City with his wife, a kindergarten teacher, and their infant daughter, to whom he writes regular letters of love, hope, advice, and anxiety on his blog, dearspike.com.

Part Two

EARLY BATTLES

The Force Is with Us. Always.

Alice Bradley

In the living room, my husband and son are killing each other.

"Zat!" cries Henry. "Zat zat zat! I got you with my lightsaber!"

"But I am your faaather . . ." Scott gasps, clutching his stomach. It's too late. Henry has gone over to the Dark Side.

There's a lot of killing going on in our house. Most of the carnage occurs on Saturday mornings, although occasionally there's time for a duel or two before school. This can be problematic, because once Henry has his dad's attention, he doesn't want to let go. "But we haven't played at aaaall," Henry will moan, even after they've been whapping at each other for the past hour. It's never enough for Henry: if he could play *Star Wars* with his dad every minute of the day, he would. He recently told me his idea of the Best Weekend Ever. "Dad and I would play *Star Wars*," he said, "for two days without stopping. We would go to sleep and wake up and still be playing *Star Wars*."

"That does sounds great," I said. I pictured Henry nudging

Scott awake with his lightsaber at 6 A.M., his Darth Vader mask affixed to his face. "We meet again," he would intone, while Scott whimpers. Maybe I could go away for the weekend while the boys enjoy their quality time? This might be the Best Weekend Ever for me, too.

"Then, at the end of the two days, you would come and bring us new toys and ice cream," he added, while checking my expression. *Was she really going to go for it?*

That pretty much sums up Henry's relationship with both of us. I'm good for toy purchasing and food-giving, but all he wants from Scott is time. Time to play *Power Rangers,* or *Invading Pirates from Space.* But mostly, time to play *Star Wars.*

Scott complains about Henry's *Star Wars* obsession, which I find hilarious. I had to endure a great deal of George Lucas's creations well before Henry came into being. When I met Scott twelve years ago, he identified himself right away as a die-hard fan. "It's sort of my thing," he had told me, if not on the first date, then shortly thereafter. "I'm very into it." He warned me, and I dated him anyway. I simply didn't consider what "very into" meant. I thought it meant that if someone mentioned *Star Wars,* he'd reply, "Ah, yes, know it well." Perhaps a wistful look would come over him. Maybe he had a few *Star Wars*–related books. As an aspiring filmmaker, he doubtlessly admired George Lucas, and I could respect that. But it ended there, I assumed.

You will note the ominous foreshadowing.

But then I learned. There were the twenty-year-old home movies: Scott and his best friend reenacting the deadly standoff between Han Solo and Greedo. Scott leaping and tripping around his backyard, a lightsaber hand-etched into the film.

And it didn't end there. I learned that Scott still turned *Star Wars* on "as background noise" whenever he worked, or cleaned, or ate, or sat. That he read *Star Wars* fan sites every morning and evening. That if he happened to be flipping through the channels and *Star Wars* was on, he *had to watch it*. That he was currently building a few models of *Star Wars* ships. And he worked on them while watching, yes, *Star Wars*.

It's not that I loathed *Star Wars*, at least not at first, but I had never been all that enthusiastic about it. I wanted to be Princess Leia just as much as any typical girl in the 1970s. But then I moved on. I wanted to be Wonder Woman. Then Mary Tyler Moore. I developed an obsession with Garfield. The usual stuff. That *I grew out of.*

And yet, despite *Star Wars,* we continued to date. We moved in together. I didn't move out, even when in the intervening years George Lucas had decided to reissue the *Star Wars* trilogy with updated effects, because he hates me, and then— what the hell!—create a NEW trilogy, because he really hates me. I watched a lot of *Star Wars* in those years. All for Scott.

But I still loved him, damn it, and we forged ahead with our own trilogy: "First Comes Love, then Comes Marriage: The Reckoning." Thus did our son, Henry, come into being.

Henry was born in October 2002. "I can't wait until the first time he watches *Star Wars,*" Scott said to me during one of our first days at home. He was looking down at our seven-pound lump of innocence, his mind unblemished by Lucasian mythology. "Can you believe *he doesn't know about* Star Wars *yet?* It's going to be amazing."

"I know, and can you imagine how great it will be if you wait until he's the same age you were when it came out? Then it would be like this special rite of passage for him. You were, what, six? Definitely we should wait until then. Man! That's going to be something!" I said, trying to muster up a little enthusiasm.

Scott saw right through me. "Six years? You really think I'm going to wait six *years*? If he could hold his head up, I'd show it to him right now."

"The years will fly by. I bet you won't even notice how long it's been."

"I'd be surprised if I can wait two years."

"Scott. A two-year-old can't watch *Star Wars*. It's not *age-appropriate*." I had just learned about things being *age-appropriate* and liked to pull it out, to show that I knew about child-rearing.

"Three years, then. I can fast-forward through the violent parts, you know. It's not like he'd notice."

I made a lot of noise about not liking *Star Wars,* but the truth is, I love my husband, and my husband loves *Star Wars,* and I like it when he's happy. If Henry fell as hard for *Star Wars* as Scott did, I thought, it would make Scott happier than if he were doing quadratic equations in pre-K. I actually worried that Henry might grow up to be a boy for whom *Star Wars* did *not* make any particular impression. Maybe he'd prefer playing cowboy, or dental hygienist. Perhaps he would suffer from a delicate constitution, and space scenes would make him vertiginous. Instead, he'd enjoy spending his afternoons sketching elaborate designs for women's footwear. Maybe he'd enjoy *lacrosse*. What would Scott do with a son like that?

I soon discovered that I had nothing to worry about. One December morning, two years into Henry's life, Scott sat our son on the couch and played a few minutes of *Star Wars* for him. Until that point, Henry was your typical truck-loving toddler. He would look at books about space, but was far more interested in, say, articulated crash rescue vehicles.

Just a few minutes of *Star Wars* would change all that.

As was our custom, I was sleeping while Scott took the morning shift. I wasn't there for Henry's transformation to Rabid *Star Wars* Fan. I'm not sure what annoyed me more: that Scott was showing him a movie we had agreed to wait on, or that I didn't get to see his face at his moment of discovery. No matter: This was his dad's thing, and his dad got to be there for it. When I walked into the room, they were both huddled together on the couch, beaming. "Don't get mad, I'm just showing him Yoda," Scott told me. There was Yoda hobbling about, messing with syntax, doing what Yoda does. The scene ended, and Scott turned off the television. Henry was pointing at the set, as if Yoda had been permanently imprinted on the blank screen. "What was THAT," he said. His favorite Tonka Truck fell off his lap. He didn't notice. Scott said, "I think he liked it!"

Henry couldn't stop talking about Yoda all morning, then all day, then all week. Scott does an excellent Yoda, and I do not. Henry wanted to hear Yoda. Often. Thus was Scott called upon, frequently, often while at work, to utter such grand statements as "My best pal, you are," and "Eat your green beans, you will." It was my job, according to my son, to conjure up tales of him and Yoda sharing adventures. I tried to transform Yoda into an upstanding model of toy sharing and peaceful snack negotiations. Henry cut me off. He was not interested in my useless morality tales. Only his father understood what he needed: *more Star Wars.*

Then, one fateful day, Scott headed down to the basement

and brought up his beloved *Star Wars* lunch box. It was dented and broken, the hinges no longer functioning, wrapped in masking tape to keep the two parts together. A label was taped across the top: FIGURES. Henry danced around Scott as he pried the box open. The top popped off, and there was every known character from the *Star Wars* universe. Princess Leia. Luke Skywalker. Darth Vader. Han Solo. Han Solo in Hoth battle gear. Boba Fett. Death Star Engineer #6. And ships, too: X-wings and A-wings and B-wings; every variety of wing that existed was crammed into that tin lunch box. "Maybe we could give him just a few of these?" I said, but it was useless. Henry was already elbow-deep in the lunch box, hyperventilating. "What do you think, buddy?" Scott said, but he could barely hear us.

I fought the intrusion of all this *Star Wars* paraphernalia for a while—Couldn't we have waited? Wasn't he too young for it? Didn't most toddlers still watch *Bob the Builder*, or adventures involving potty time?—but it was no use. It didn't matter if we never bought another *Star Wars* toy; Henry's Fisher Price gas station morphed into the Death Star and his tea set became the *Millennium Falcon*. Scott went to work, and I was left alone with Henry's incessant questions regarding ancillary *Star Wars* characters I had never heard of. Right from the beginning I assumed the role of ignoramus. No way I was going to get roped into this. "I have no idea who Bib Fortuna or Bell Biv Devoe or whoever is," I said. "Let's call your father."

And so it has gone, for the past two years since Henry's introduction to the world of George Lucas. Sure, he's since enjoyed the company of other men: Superman, Yellow Power

Ranger, the Decepticons. But he'll always be a *Star Wars* fan, because that's his connection to his father. And there is no end to the universe of *Star Wars* entertainment matter. When they ran out of films to watch, there were books; when they read the books to tatters, there were fan sites, animations, short videos. Almost every morning they find something to watch online. It doesn't matter to Henry how bad it is, as long as lightsabers are prominently figured, and he can sit on his dad's lap while he watches.

These days, according to Henry, only Scott can play *Star Wars* right, and I consider this to be an excellent development. This is payback for my years of conjugal loyalty despite my now searing hatred of George Lucas and all he has wrought. I have been known to exaggerate my cluelessness in order to encourage this line of thinking in Henry. I was told long ago that I didn't play *Star Wars* correctly because I talked about *feelings*, so now I'm sure to mention some character's emotion the moment my butt hits the carpet. "Let's play Darth Vader Is Sad Because No One Likes Him!" I say, and am abruptly exiled from the playroom, forced to read a book by myself or enjoy a hot bath while Scott gets to rebuild the Death Star.

Despite how much Henry clearly worships him, Scott feels guilty much of the time. Guilty that he has to work late, guilty that he's not doing enough for Henry or that what he's doing, he's not doing right. He can't give Henry all the time he demands, and as he nears five, Henry's demands are increasing by the day. No human being can give Henry what he really wants, which is for time to stop so that he and his dad can lose themselves in an alternate universe, one where their lightsabers really work and their best friend is a Wookiee.

> *No human being can give Henry what he really wants, which is for time to stop so that he and his dad can lose themselves in an alternate universe, one where their light sabers really work and their best friend is a Wookiee.*

Scott can't always be here, but when he is, he's up for anything his son proposes, time (and space/time continuum) permitting. And Henry knows it. When Scott's at work, I watch Henry plotting new adventures for them to play upon his return. Because Scott is a film editor, Henry understands that his father "makes movies," so now Henry plans the movies *he'll* be making as a grown-up. At bedtime he tells Scott all about his newest idea. "It's called *Return of the Empire, Strike Three: Galaxy of The Jedi.*" (We hope that George Lucas doesn't sue him for plagiarism.) More than anything, more than being a Jedi, Henry wants to be just like his dad. So he must be doing something right.

Alice Bradley is the author of the blog Finslippy. Hailed as "the greatest of the mommy blogs" by the National Review Online, *Finslippy has also been featured in* Redbook, *the* Oakland Tribune, *the* Newark Star-Ledger, *and* The New York Times. *Alice has an M.F.A. in writing from the New School University, and her fiction has appeared in several literary journals. She lives with her husband, son, cat, and dog in New Jersey.*

Day Job

Heather B. Armstrong

When my daughter Leta was twenty-one months old, my husband, Jon, quit his office job to become her primary caregiver. I had been the stay-at-home parent until that point, but my freelance work started to bring in a salary equivalent to his. So we looked at our finances, made a few adjustments, and then Jon became the stay-at-home dad.

At first I had a hard time adjusting because I had a system that I used to make sure the house ran smoothly, and Jon's lumbering body was like a huge wrench being thrown into my machinery. When he took over some of the chores, I didn't like the way he did them. He was too slow, or he didn't wipe the counters in the right direction, and it took me a long time to come to terms with the fact that it's okay if he doesn't do things my way even though my way is the right way, the superior way.

Even though I was suddenly overwhelmed with the pressure of being the breadwinner for my family, I was much more relieved to have the constant companionship of someone who spoke Adult. During the sometimes lonely months that I stayed at home with Leta, I spent many afternoons making up excuses to go to the grocery store so that I could have a conversation with the teenage cashier.

Having my husband at home also came with many other added benefits, like not having to be the primary diaper changer, and having someone else around to answer to the constant drone of an immobile child. It also meant that I'd get to use the bathroom by myself. For almost two years I had been sharing the bathroom with a monkey-like intruder who routinely ingested tampons and scaled my perched body like a roach up a wall. Never again would I take for granted the ability to wipe my butt with no one sitting at my feet and assessing my technique.

And despite the relief I felt at having him home, in those first few months of our new arrangement I began to believe that husbands and wives, mothers and the fathers of their children, we were not meant to live like this, together with no mileage between us. He was there *all the time* and he was constantly doing things the wrong way.

For instance, he didn't drive the right way to the grocery store, a place where stay-at-home parents spend half of their lives. I had always admired the way he drove on the freeway, aggressively and at thrillingly illegal speed. But on surface streets he'd morph into a silver-haired invalid who could barely see over the steering wheel, someone who couldn't seem to remember the name of that nice man who, back in 1945, used to trim his hedges, and maybe if he stared out the side window long enough it would come to him. The usual five-minute drive to the store would turn into a three-day epic journey. He hadn't been a stay-at-home father long enough to understand that he could better use that time to sleep on the couch while the baby watched Cinemax.

He also talked, a lot, all the time without stopping, ever. When he and I first started dating, I found this habit very endearing. It didn't necessarily lose its charm, but I definitely had to get used to it again. I enjoyed the fully formed words and complete sentences, but just like our daughter's incoherent rambling, all those excess consonants and vowels tended to echo like noises through the Grand Canyon, repeating, repeating, going on forever, bouncing off the walls of eternity. Suddenly I found myself yearning for silence, hoping that he might take up thumb-sucking.

And then there was the laundry. Jon had a talent for turning two small loads of dirty clothes into a six-day project. I normally divided everything into either lights or darks and could have a week's worth of clothes washed and folded within an afternoon. But he had different ideas, complicated theories about laundry detergent, and he believed that every color of clothing needed its own load. Reds were only washed with reds, browns with browns, yellows with yellows, and sometimes an entire load of laundry was made up of a pair of socks. He also dried *everything,* including my sports bra, and I remember one particular workout when I lost feeling in both legs because my circulation was being cut off at my boobs.

Jon approached household chores with an urgency very different than mine: none. And that was more than a little infuriating, but I soon realized that he didn't need to develop that particular part of his process because he had in me a backup mechanism. When I was alone with our daughter, every chore seemed to hinge on whether or not the one right before it got done. Suddenly there were four hands where there were once only two, so Shit Could Get Done simultaneously. Chores were being accomplished *at the same time*. I wouldn't be lying if I said that from the perspective of a woman who had been doing all the chores by herself for almost two years, this was the equivalent of really awesome sex.

The breadth and magnitude of Jon's domestic journey can be demonstrated in various episodes, the first one involving his butt and a chocolate muffin. Just a few months after Jon took over as primary caregiver, we took a trip to Texas, and while waiting to depart, Jon accidentally sat on a chocolate muffin. The fudge-like consistency of the melted chocolate chips formed a peculiar shape on the seat of his khaki pants. Instead of asking me to scrub his butt for him—and recording it to sell on eBay—he asked me for a wet wipe from my purse. Five minutes later he returned from the airport restroom looking as if his existence had never collided with that of the chocolate muffin. The stain was gone and in its place was a perfectly clean stretch of khaki fabric. I nearly choked on my disbelief. My husband was a stain-remover, a *chocolate* stain-remover, an *improvisational* stain-remover. I couldn't have been more surprised if he had shot that chocolate muffin out of his butt.

The second instance happened after an intense day of housecleaning about a month after that trip to Texas. I had spent the morning straightening up the front part of the house and then took over playing with Leta while Jon finished up the kitchen and bathroom. Each surface in those two rooms required its own brand of cleaner, and while I had been very specific about certain surfaces like the granite countertops, I let him figure out his own process for everything else. As we were getting ready for bed, I noticed Jon inspecting the work he had done earlier, looking over the toilet and the tiles on the floor. "I can't tell you," he said, "how much I love that Comet spray cleanser." Really? Because I can't tell you how hot that makes me.

> *As we were getting ready for bed, I noticed Jon inspecting the work he had done earlier, looking over the toilet and the tiles on the floor. "I can't tell you," he said, "how much I love that Comet spray cleanser." Really? Because I can't tell you how hot that makes me.*

Recently, Jon gave me the most valuable gift a wife and mother could ever hope for: validation.

I remember one Saturday afternoon when our daughter was ten months old, when Jon was still working his office job, how he informed me that he'd be spending the afternoon painting the fence in the backyard.

"How long do you think it will take?" I asked, having longed for a break all week, the baby clinging to my neck.

"Not sure," he said. "Maybe an hour?"

Three hours later I marched back outside, the baby still cradled in my arms, and clomped over to the fence. "Your hour is up," I proclaimed. And then I shoved the baby into his right arm, the same one that was holding a dripping paintbrush.

For months afterward he thought I had had an episode, a sudden panic attack, and he referred to that afternoon as that one time I was so stressed out that I couldn't let him finish the fence. Which is funny, because I remember it as that one time I was so in control of myself that I didn't kill my husband.

And then a few weeks ago on a Saturday afternoon, I left the house to take the dog for a walk, by myself, and I had not been gone for ten minutes when I rounded the corner to see Leta and a haggard-looking Jon out looking for us.

"It's Saturday," he said as he approached. "I really need you to stick around the house to help me out. I need the break."

"Are you having a bad day?" I asked, already aware of the answer.

"Not really," he said. "It's just, I don't know, *this is hard.*"

That one admission, that tiny sentence, made me realize that in everything he was doing—from his inability to drive anywhere in less than a decade, to the incessant rambling, to his peculiar approach to laundry—he was doing his best, just like I was, to try and get through the day.

Heather B. Armstrong is the award-winning publisher of dooce®️ (dooce.com). She gained notoriety in 2002 as one of the first people to be fired because of a blog, and in 2005 dooce.com was chosen by Time *magazine as one of the 50 Coolest Websites. Armstrong has been on* Good Morning America, CNN, NPR, *and* ABC's World News Tonight *as a featured commenter on both blogging and post-partum depression, as well as profiled in* The New York Times Sunday Style *section and the* Washington Post Weekend Magazine. *She was published in* Real Simple's *Family edition in August 2007. Armstrong lives in Salt Lake City, Utah, with her husband, daughter, and dog.*

The Last Summer

Doug French

Dear Boys:

Hello from August 2007, in New York City. As I write this, you're only five and two, ages best kept for punctuating your speech with words like *idiot* and *poopie,* respectively. So this letter isn't meant as much for the current you as it is for Future You, who live in the Marvelous World of Tomorrow. Or in a Scorched, Dystopian Hellscape, depending on which movies you believe. How is the future anyway? Is this "book" a rare relic of a bygone age? Are you thinking back to a simpler, pastoral time, before all information was shared wirelessly using osmotic Google MemBrains™ affixed to your temples? Are *The Simpsons* still cranking out new episodes?

Back here in 2007, the last few months have been pretty sweet. I work as a teacher, so I've been off work since the middle of June and home with you as the family's primary boytender. And for the past ten weeks, the three of us have shared a wondrous and rare opportunity: the chance to wake up every day in New York City and ask ourselves, "What'll we do today?"

The answer is, a helluva lot. We played about 1,000 innings

of dingerball (which is what baseball would be like if the only possible hit were a home run). We went to the aquarium, the zoos, the museums, the water parks. We took swim lessons. We explored the distant planet Freezo (a.k.a., the fridge) with our LEGO battle cruisers. We read books, drew pictures, watched a few bajillion episodes of *Dirty Jobs,* and built Rube Goldberg contraptions out of dryer tubes and duct tape and TwoBert's board books, lined up like dominos. We baked a chocolate cake, for Chrissakes.

There were also momentous events. TwoBert started using the potty, quasi-reliably. A-Rod hit his 500th home run at Yankee Stadium, and we were there, four rows off the field. We saw Lexington Avenue blow up.

But now the summer is winding down, and in a few days Robert will start kindergarten. Every parent knows that the first child's first day of school is a big deal, because the Summer Before Kindergarten is the valediction of pure childhood, before alarm clocks and homework and peer pressure and girl-cooties start peeing in the rain barrel. When you drop the "pre" from preschool, it's a matter of time before the onset of . . . *tweenerhood.* Barf, already.

> *Every parent knows that the first child's first day of school is a big deal, because the Summer Before Kindergarten is the valediction of pure childhood, before alarm clocks and homework and peer pressure and girlcooties.*

When this summer adventure started, I knew it would be special. And I was grateful to be around to share so much of it, because after school starts, our relationships will change.

Robert will get a swift boost of emotional independence, and TwoBert will spend days alone with a sitter, and our special dynamic won't be as blissfully unfettered as it is now.

Unfortunately, the new fetteration goes deeper than that. We're about to get much more fettered. Big time. Because last Thanksgiving, almost ten months ago, your mom and I decided to get divorced. So this will be the last summer that the Three French Men will be full-time roommates.

I know what you're thinking. Ten months? Seriously? Wouldn't someone normally have moved out by now? But this is not normal. This is Manhattan, the billionaires' playground, where real estate prices defy gravity and obscenely rich people can buy a penthouse quadruplex, a townhouse or two, and a little pied-à-terre for their children's horse trainers. We, on the other hand, have had enough of an adventure staying afloat with one rent, let alone two. Divorce is a long process, and we're working on it as prudently and diligently as possible. In the meantime, here I am, living in an 800-square-foot apartment, with my two favorite people in the world and the one who used to be.

It's a peculiar moment when you pause to regard your life's path and wonder just how in the blue blazes you got where you are. One minute you're young and single, enjoying freewheeling, free-balling, free-and-easy freedom as a freelancer. The next you're more than just a SAHD; you're a Salaried, Emotionally-Separated-but-Empirically-Cohabitating, Stay-at-Home Father of Two (a distinction that, as of this writing, lacks a media-friendly acronym). On paper, it sounds like hell on earth. And it was. But after all this is over, I strangely feel like I'm going to be much better off.

Don't get me wrong. Divorce is awful. When it all hit the fan last fall, my whole body went numb for about a week. I managed to maintain my schedule, shuffling from A to B per usual, but I swear if you'd popped me across the face with a textbook, I wouldn't have felt a thing.

I spent the next few months feeling every possible emotion all at once, and it was exhausting. I'd work through the day distractedly, come home to see you off to bed, then head to the coffee shop around the corner, open my laptop, and pour off all the wastewater that had accumulated in my brain gutters during the day. I swilled coffee and speed-typed and purged everything into one huge file that comprises 45 single-spaced pages and just over 30,000 words. And no, you can't read it, because it is such a caustic brew of bile and misery that, for the sake of world safety, it should be sealed in a block of galvanized bauxite and shot into space. It suffices to say that the overriding theme touches on three central points:

1. My wife is a very objectionable person.
2. I am a very objectionable person.
3. Existence is inherently unpleasant.

Trying to keep things civil in front of you two was an adventure early on, because it was so easy for raw emotions to boil over. We were like two pit bulls in a bathtub, struggling for traction and barking away our frustrations. When tempers ran high, we usually ran to the opposite end of the apartment and launched into bouts of screaming stage whispers. They were horrendous back then, but they seem pretty comical now, from a distance. We must have looked pretty damn ridiculous, two people ensnared in a fit of furious quiet. What you can't express with volume, you make up for with Force! Ful! Ges! Tic! U! La! Tions!

Like I said. Comical.

Months have passed, and your mom and I have gotten better at making the best of a crappy situation, mostly by avoiding each other. We keep it together pretty well around you because we get to air it out with a couples therapist, a very nice man who gets paid piles of cash to sit there and nod at us. Occasionally, he crosses his legs. Or interjects with something like, "When she said that, what did you hear?" It's a nice racket, if you don't mind spending your days submerged in anguished bickering.

We haven't yet told you, officially, that we're splitting up, but you suspect something. You've definitely caught on to the fact that the four of us never do anything together. Did that seem weird to you? Or perfectly normal, given no frame of reference? I've gotten used to it, but let me tell you that walking alone with you in the park is not exactly a walk in the park. Now that TwoBert has his own opinions, and is a big fan of runningrunningrunning, keeping track of the both of you is a singular challenge. I've had to develop a sort of Iguanavision that lets my eyeballs segment and follow each of you independently. Museums are the worst, especially when they're filled to the rafters with day campers and school trippers. I've learned, therefore, to dress each of you in the most garish clothes possible. Now you know why TwoBert is always wearing that same damn rainbow shirt in all those old photos.

As the four of us inevitably transition to whatever's next, I'm glad you have each other. You guys have been thick as thieves from the start, and although beating the snot out of each other is becoming your favorite hobby, woe betide any kid who messes with either of you. Just today, while we were playing dingerball, a slack-jawed six-year-old yanked the bat out of Robert's hands and ran away with it. Robert gave chase, but it was TwoBert who made first contact and tried to run the kid over with his little stroller. He risked life and limb to protect the family's honor, and I couldn't have been prouder.

∾

Since you've shown you're willing to jeopardize body parts to defend the family name, you might as well know a bit more about it. We Frenches can trace our arrival in America to around 1635, when Richard French, a nine-year-old orphan who came over with his guardian, settled in Cambridge, Massachusetts. And in case the following gets a little confusing, here's a chart of the generations that link him to you:

    I. Richard French, 1625–1688.
   II. Joseph French, 1648–1732.
  III. Jonathan French, 1690-1777.
   IV. Josiah French, 1728–1784.
    V. Josiah French, Jr., 1765–1840.
   VI. Calvin French, 1799–1879.
  VII. George Blood French, 1836–1910.
 VIII. Wayne Martin French, 1878–1953.
   IX. George Warren French, 1905–1978.
    X. Wayne Gordon French, 1936–
   XI. Me, 1965–
  XII. You guys, 2002– and 2005–

I have some compilations of letters, court documents, and other narratives that chronicle the French family exploits over the last four centuries, and I hope someday you'll get a chance to read them, because they're a real hoot. Stepsiblings marrying? Fathers suing sons? Court dates for "bodily uncleanes" [sic] and "uncivil carriage"? We've got it all, baby.

Anyway. Richard begat Joseph, who begat Jonathan, who begat Josiah. We know a bit about them from public documents (tax rolls, wills, etc.) but we don't have much firsthand information, because amid all this begetting there wasn't a lot of writing. These men were New England farmers, who were busy with more important things. Like eating. And not freezing to death.

Josiah Junior changed all that when he and his partners built a textile mill in Proctorsville, Vermont, that revolutionized cloth-making in the region and made him a big shot. From then on, the Frenches joined the area's landed gentry, and Josiah Junior's kids could afford to put down the farm implements, wash up, and go to school.

That's when the writing started.

Josiah Junior's second son, Calvin, started out as a farmhand, but by the time he became a grandfather, he had spent 45 years as a lawyer, businessman, deputy sheriff, judge, justice of the peace, and state senator. And he wrote all about it. Letters, travel journals, memoirs, you name it. The man made Stephen King look like a haikuist.

On Christmas Eve, 1878, Calvin wrote a short note to his first grandson, Wayne Martin French, to accompany a modest passbook savings account he opened for the boy:

His grandfather, with a grateful heart, would enclose the within Christmas gift as a token of his love for the dear boy, hoping at the same time that, trifling as it is in fact, it may serve to remind the donee in after years, should his life be spared, of the necessity of caring for, and keeping small, as well as larger sums prudently invested, if he would make himself independent of his friends, and honored and respected by the community in which he may reside.

I've always admired this letter, because it conjures an image of an avuncular, self-effacing, and tirelessly prudent New Englander who could cram 86 words into one sentence. (I mentioned he was a lawyer, right?) He may also have been thinking of his own mortality, since he died the following year.

Calvin's son, George Blood French, was a remarkable man, not least because he was the first in the line with a middle name. (And what a middle name! *Blood!* I wish I could tell you it was a valorous nickname bestowed by the regiments that served under him in the Civil War, but it's just his mother's maiden name. Still, it occurred to me to give one of you *Blood* as a middle name, because nobody on the playground is gonna mess with a kid named *Blood.* But I thought better of it.)

After his father died, George Blood and his magnificent handlebar moustache moved to Fremont, Nebraska, for a taste of "a more active life." By the time he became a grandfather, however, Wayne Martin had moved back East, to New Jersey. George Blood knew he wouldn't see his new grandson, George Warren, all that much, so he followed Calvin's example and wrote a note to *his* grandson on *his* first Christmas. And a tradition was born.

Every first grandson since then has been born in the New York area, and each has received a letter from his grandfather on his first Christmas. Wayne Martin wrote to Dad, Grandpa wrote to me, and Dad wrote to Robert.

Which brings me, quite laboriously, to my purpose.

This letter-writing tradition means very much to me, because of the special relationships I've had with my dad and grandfather. Grandpa was the first best friend I ever had. When I was in grade school, he and Grandma lived across the street from us, and I spent many afternoons over at their place, shooting hoops and eating everything that wasn't tied down. And some stuff that was.

We moved away in the summer of 1977, and five months later, on Super Bowl Sunday, Grandpa died of a heart attack. For months I missed him terribly, and the following summer, when the grown-ups gathered to scatter his ashes in his favorite river, I had to stay home. The boat was too small, they said, and if they invited me, they'd have to invite all the grandkids. Which to me was total bullshit, because I was the oldest, and I knew him best, and if the other grandkids couldn't go, then tough shit on them. I think I cried more that day than on the day he died.

Dad and I have always been close, and by now I'm sure Future You have heard my favorite story, about how he came down to college my fourth year and told me how proud of me he was, a billion times. So I'll spare you here.

I want very badly to continue this tradition, and I hope I'll be able to, should you be lucky enough to have your own kids, and should I be lucky enough to meet them. But life is fickle, and I'm already forty-two, and my marriage will be the first in 129 years to end in divorce. If I die tomorrow, you might never know much about me or the sundry history behind your surname. So for now, I want you to have this letter to pass on to my grandchildren, if/when they come along.

Now, I don't want this to turn into some Polonious-and-Laertes screed about fatherly advice and neither a borrower nor lender being. And believe me—I cannot stress this enough—please do not feel pressured to procreate just to keep this tradition alive. If kids are in your plan, that's fine, and if they're not, that's fine, too. I want, above all things, for you to live your life, to the greatest extent possible, on your own terms. I want you to find a good partner in life, someone to whom you can give your heart fully. (And no offense, but I want to find one first.)

I don't want you to think that marriage is a bad thing, because it's not—as long as you do it right. Be patient and follow your heart, and don't worry if somewhere along the way somebody metaphorically rips it out of your chest and pounds it metaphorically flat with a metaphorical tire iron. It will always bounce back.

It might seem easy to write the marriage off as a mistake, but I'm trying to ease up on that word. I've spent too much of my life avoiding mistakes like the plague, and now, ironically, I've made one of the worst of all: I married the wrong person. Naturally, she didn't seem like the wrong person at the time. We had a lot of fun early on, and I thought we fit together pretty well. I've kept a bunch of pictures of the two of us in happier times, just so you don't grow up wondering just what in tarnation got us together in the first place. You can see them when you're older. Maybe.

So please, in the name of John, Paul, George, and possibly Ringo, do not be afraid to screw up once in a while. Life can beat every creative impulse out of you and make you scared to embark in new directions. I say, embark away. Case in point: The blog I started, Laid-Off Dad, was supposed to be a hobby. I spent about two seconds naming it, and all I wanted was something to help me practice writing every day. Turns out, it's helped me meet hundreds of wonderful writers and kindred spirits all over the world, and it's offered me the chance to write this to you.

At this point, I'm hoping your mom and I can build a new, coparenting relationship that is at least cordial. It seems like a remote possibility right now, since she and I are still tap-dancing around each other so hypersensitively, amid our still-unresolved negotiations. Our communications are halting and strained, because we're still working through those ornery last vestiges of resentment and anger that won't go away.

I am optimistic, though, because there is one subject that manages to cut through the ice and lets us laugh together, and it's you. The other day, after you went to bed, I told your mom how Robert and I were on the subway platform, and I told him which track the express train ran on. And he looked at me incredulously and said, "Dad, I'm a New Yorker! I know how the world works!" Little stuff like that just rips us to pieces, and lets us know that no marriage can be a complete failure if it produces kids like you.

So maybe your mom and I will each find happiness with

new people, and maybe you'll be able to pattern your romantic lives on two good relationships, rather than one that sorta stunk. It could happen. Right?

For me, the worst part is Not Knowing, because Not Knowing is the thing that keeps me Not Sleeping. I don't know how all this will play out. I don't know where we're all going to live. I don't know if I can afford to keep the job I love. Worst of all, I don't know how the divorce will affect you. Have you become sullen punk-nihilists? Or Promise Keepers? Or both? Have we managed to keep a close relationship? Or do you hate my guts?

What I do know is that your mom and I aren't in love anymore. Instead, I'm in love with the image of an intact family unit, the kind that every kid deserves and that I wish I could provide for you. But after months of introspection and pain and therapy, I know that divorce is unfortunately the only path left. I'm disappointed and sad, but I know I've done everything in my power to try to save the marriage, and that gives me some peace of mind.

I also know that this divorce has absolutely nothing to do with you. I know that you boys are the best things that ever happened to me, and that the Three French Men will always be family. I know that I will move heaven and earth to be as much a part of your lives as you'll let me, and I know I will always be nearby, to love and support you, until the day I die.

And if your kids want to come to my funeral, you better damn well bring 'em.

Love,
Dad

Doug French's two favorite pastimes are writing and being a dad. After he lost his job in 2003, he started his blog, Laid-Off Dad, to find humor amid the stress and penury. Then Parents *magazine found him, newspapers interviewed him, and readers chose LOD as the Best Daddy Blog in the "Best of Blogs" awards for 2005. Currently biding his time between layoffs, Doug lives in New York City. He is balding and nearsighted, but otherwise awesome.*

Long Live the Weeds and the Wilderness Yet

James Griffioen

My hands were bleeding after the pack of wild dogs attacked us. I only noticed in the car, studying them tense around the wheel as they guided us through the streets of Detroit. For a moment I suspected new wounds, pain still obscured by adrenaline. Blood was trickling down the backs of both hands, though I was sure I hadn't been bitten. The dogs had gotten no closer than the stick I'd used to smash one across the face. During all that thrashing, I must have aggravated old wounds on my hands that had been there since the previous weekend, which I spent scraping away decades-old wallpaper with a wide trowel while preparing to paint our bedroom walls seafoam green. Misuse of the trowel had left several deep centimeter-long gashes in the arcs between my fingers, wounds that should have healed, and would have, had it not been for the tension in my fists when fighting off the feral dogs.

When I realized these were old wounds, I was immediately ashamed by the subsiding flash of pride. I was reminded of the time a gang of teenagers mugged me in a San Francisco housing project, leaving me kicked and battered on the sidewalk. I didn't even fight back. That night, I walked home to look in the mirror, strangely proud of my puffed-up cheek, proud of my neck and shirt covered in blood from the wound in my lip. *Who is that?* I asked. *Surely that's not me.* I refused to clean myself up. My girlfriend was not home, and I wanted her to see it. What a shameful way to end up feeling so alive.

The blood on my hands was nearly dry by the time we got back to our tree-lined neighborhood on Detroit's east side. As we pulled into our driveway, I considered the overall dryness of my hands after a long winter, the blood, the flakes of paint and sawdust in my hair and beard, and felt for a moment like the kind of man who could get into a conversation about stock car racing or a tattoo on my bicep honoring a good friend who died in a motorcycle accident. Then I unbuckled and lifted my two-year-old daughter out of her car seat, carried her into the house, and fixed macaroni and cheese with sliced hot dogs before putting her down for a nap. You see, I am not at all that kind of man. I am a stay-at-home dad.

A year before, I had been a fourth-year securities litigator at a big San Francisco law firm. I had my own office with a view of the Bay Bridge. I wore Italian suits and shook hands with bank presidents. Since then I have let my hair grow long and wear T-shirts every day, showering rarely. Were old colleagues to see me, they might wonder if I've gone insane, or if perhaps I'm participating in some bizarre Babylonian ritual of mourning. But this is not a story of failure, or some mesmerizing fall from grace. I willingly took this plunge, willingly left a partnership-track position and moved my family to the heart of the second-most-dangerous city in America, all because I decided what I wanted to do with my life was to be a better dad. I wanted to teach my daughter the same things I had to unlearn after years spent as a corporate lawyer: that soul is more important than money, that love means more than material things. Detroit, I figured, was as good a place as any to start.

> *I wanted to teach my daughter the same things I had to unlearn after years spent as a corporate lawyer: that soul is more important than money, that love means more than material things.*

I am part of a generation of men who are proving themselves comfortable with taking a more active—or even equal—role in parenting. I don't usually mind telling people what I do, because more often than not, other men have something positive to say about it. "That sounds so great," they say. Or, "You're so lucky. I would give anything to go back and spend those years with my kids." More and more men, it seems, are open about admitting that they would like the opportunity to do what I do, or regretting that they never did anything like it. Still, at every cocktail party, wedding, or funeral there is someone who doesn't get it, someone who clearly thinks it's a little weird. And for as much as I believe that being here all day, every day for my kid makes me a better father than I had been as a busy lawyer, there is that nagging, primal idea of the father as provider. Here I am, freshly thirty years old, a parent of a two-year-old with another one on the way. I should be burdened by the heft of responsibility. I should be losing my hair, padding my 401(k), and starting college-savings plans. I should be billing hours in some office somewhere, not sitting around playing all day long. That's not just my own father's voice talking, but some deeply ingrained cultural imperative. Men work.

They provide. They put meat on the table. Men have ambition. They seek power. They don't consider a four-mile jog, an enormous sandcastle, and a clean kitchen to be acceptable accomplishments for a weekday. Occasionally, whenever I find myself developing a preference for one household cleaner over another, or when I feel a swell of pride at the ponytails I've put in my daughter's hair, I wait for the wife to get home from work and then I sneak down into the basement to put in a DVD with Gary Cooper or Steve McQueen just so I can remember what it looks like to be a real man. If I'm feeling really emasculated, I'll put in a DVD with Gene Kelly, because sometimes the only cure for feeling like less of a man is to watch another man dance.

My own father is a real man, from the way he drinks at least half a gallon of milk every day, right from the carton, to the way he takes off his shirt to mow the lawn even when it's not all that hot outside. He works with his hands, repairing antique cars for a living. He's had his nose broken and several fingers cut off in work accidents. The fingers were reattached, though they remain dead-looking, purple and bloated. Several times over the years he called me from emergency rooms to tell me he'd just driven himself across town to the hospital with one of his fingers sitting in a cup full of ice in his lap. I never took any interest in his cars. I never saw him reading a book, so I read everything I could get my hands on. He never cared much for school, or went to college. You can definitely see the mark of my filial rebellion in my hands. I have soft, college-boy hands. They have never hammered steel into a fender, or sandblasted the doors of a 1955 Mercedes-Benz 300SL Gullwing Coupe. My hands have translated ancient Greek poetry, turned countless pages, taken the California bar, and written lengthy legal briefs on the application of the unclean-hands doctrine to trustees representing bankrupt entities. I am a man whose work with his hands generally begins and ends at a keyboard. I rebelled against my father by becoming a goddamn wuss.

My father always said he hated cities. Since I left the protection of the roof he provided, I have always lived in one, though I was raised in the country. Growing up, we had to live somewhere with tolerant or poorly enforced zoning laws, because my father worked in the auto body shop he built in our backyard. My childhood was spent wandering with my dog through the woods around our house, cutting across fields dotted with bales of hay, ducking through barbed wire to get to the pine forests beyond.

One of the things I love about living in the city of Detroit is that it satisfies some desire I have to return to the country. Today, several decades after the near-complete abandonment of the city by white people, many of the homes they left have burned. Some fires were set through mayhem; for years the night before Halloween has been known as Devil's Night, when arsonists wander the streets setting fire to abandoned buildings, and during the 1980s, as many as eight hundred vacant and occupied properties were lost every year as the fires spread. Sometimes fires were set by conscientious neighbors looking to rid their blocks of dilapidated eyesores used by squatters, drug addicts, and prostitutes. Either way, the charred timbers fell, collapsing into basements, eventually leaving acre after acre of urban prairie, overgrown with grasses and marauding nonnative bushes and trees. Of those abandoned buildings that have not burned or collapsed, few have been able to stave off the destructive patience of nature. Roots split masonry. Seeds germinate in the plaster that rots in the paths of sunlight shining through the broken windowpanes of ruined art deco office buildings. There are trees growing on the roofs of abandoned skyscrapers, themselves filled with roosting pigeons and raccoons who scavenge the overgrown alleyways and illegal dumping sites for nourishment. I have been told there is more vacant or abandoned property within the city limits of Detroit than there is land in San Francisco. In other words, you could move the entire city of San Francisco onto the vacant land in Detroit. There are homes here so engulfed by wildness and vacancy, when viewing them from a distance you can convince yourself you are not in one of America's largest metropolitan areas, but standing instead in the silence of some distant Western prairie. When I moved to Detroit, I started reading Hawthorne again, with his Puritan's idea of wildness as a place for wolves and demons. How many buildings did I have to see it conquer before I started believing nature had it in for us? At the very least, living in Detroit teaches us of nature's naked indifference, or perhaps, even worse, that nature holds us in complete contempt. Here, among the ruins of a modern metropolis, surrounded by the realities of the postindustrial world, we rouse pheasants in our walks along the river. In our wanderings we have encountered wild turkeys, hawks, vultures, bats, opossums, a coyote loping down an alleyway, and even a pair of white-tailed deer grazing along an abandoned railway line. I have heard the rumor that foxes, too, have returned. There are cities where the blab of the pave has silenced the voice of nature; in Detroit we are reminded that even in such places, nature's murmur remains, like the rivers that flow underground.

Growing up, I watched the rural character of my own home succumb to the consumptive demands of a nearby city. Fields became subdivisions full of cookie-cutter homes, treeless quarter-acre slices of American dream. Whole farms became big-box retail stores and their vast parking lots. In metro Detroit, for half a century, fleeing whites have sought to conquer rural areas farther and farther from the city they feared; meanwhile, the city itself has become more and more rural. It can take nearly an hour of driving to get out of suburbia before you see true country. When a father in an inner-ring Detroit suburb tells his kids he's going to bring a misbehaving dog to a farm where he'll be happier, it can take far longer to drive to true farmland than it does to drive into the green, trash-strewn fields of Detroit. That's why so many dogs get dumped here. Our own, a seemingly purebred German shorthaired pointer, was found ragged and cold wandering the streets of Detroit last winter, dumped, we speculate, by a bird hunter who discovered the dog was gun-shy. This is a partial explanation for the wandering packs of wild dogs that have become such a problem in the Motor City. Detroit is the kind of place where it seems no one will ever notice if you add just one more problem.

When we moved here, we were warned to watch out for random gunfire. A partner at my old law firm joked that he should take out an insurance policy on my life. My father was nearly as upset about our move to Detroit as he and my mother were about my decision to stay home and take care of my daughter. In Detroit, they said, a stray bullet is as likely to kill you as cancer, as a car accident. Move to the suburbs, they said. The schools will be better, too. It was noon on a startlingly warm January day when the dogs attacked us. We were at a playground on Belle Isle, the 982-acre Olmsted-designed park situated in the middle of the Detroit River. We were completely alone, not a car or another person in sight. The pack was hunting us, five of them I could count, three in front and two between us and the car. They had approached us in silence. These dogs were completely feral, mutts so severely inbred they seemed to have created their own noxious breed: one that would engage you in banjo fingerpicking duels and then jerk away from your outstretched hand; catch you unawares, inspect your teeth, and expect you to squeal. Before my brain even recognized the danger, my hands had swept my daughter from the ground, up into the elevated crook of my arm. Several of the dogs crept closer, snarling and barking. I stood there poised and alert, waiting for a further cue from the pack to propel me to fly or fight. "What are those doggies saying?" my daughter asked, oblivious to our peril.

"Those are mean doggies," I said, placing her high on a piece of playground equipment that no dog would be able to climb. "Very mean doggies." The pack advanced a bit while I had my back turned. I scanned the ground for anything to put between us. The playground was littered with trash and debris: potato chip wrappers, empty juice boxes, newspapers. I found a couple decent-sized rocks that felt heavy in my hand. "You stay there," I told my baby. "Don't move," I ordered with a seriousness she had never seen in me, resulting in unquestioning compliance. I prepared our defense. This steep slide was our last refuge. This ladder, our Alamo. I picked up a heavy fallen

branch from a few paces away, twisting off the terminal twigs
as I backed up to the slide. The dogs took another opportunity
to advance. They were close now. I chucked a rock at one and
missed, threw another and nailed it right at the base of its neck.
The dog looked shocked and stopped. The others watched us
almost casually, tongues lolling. I focused on the one closest to
us, the biggest and the meanest, clearly the alpha male. I growled
right back at him and shouted with truculence I didn't know I
could command. I charged a bit at him with the branch, bash-
ing it first against a picnic table for effect, a dervish on offense,
screaming and snarling as though I were more ferocious than
any of these creatures several litters out from anyone's living
room. I wasn't sure if any of this was what I was supposed to be
doing; my only knowledge of how to fight off a wild dog pack
came from reading Jack London's oeuvre twenty years earlier.
And I never read *White Fang* thinking its lessons would one
day apply to my own life.

My daughter was right behind me still, safe seven or more
feet in the air. The alpha male was just a few yards away now,
barking and growling in that low dangerous loop, knots of
saliva dancing from its jaw. He was not a large creature, but I
saw hints of pit bull and rottweiler diluted in his pedigree, the
kinds of dogs people buy to protect their homes and then
dump when they bite a child. I held my left arm out at him as
bait, knowing he would grab it and not want to let go, leaving
my right arm to attack. I swung the timber again and bashed
him in the jaw. He relented and sank on his haunches. In a
rage, I swung the branch wildly at two of his companions. If
the alpha had taken a step farther, I was ready to boot him in
the head, whale on him further with the stick, grab his jaws

with my bloody hands, and smash his skull against the ground. I would have had no problem killing him had he taken one step closer to my daughter: I was so tense and angry in those seconds I surely would have found some way to rip my way through his skin and throbbing viscera to pull out his rotten heart and squeeze the worms from it to show the other dogs I fucking meant business.

I'm sure I looked quite absurd.

But it worked. Apparently the wild canines of Detroit do not have a finely tuned sense of absurdity. They bought my act, slinking back a dozen yards, turning to snarl at me, and then trotted away farther until they'd crossed a stream of raw sewage. I continued to growl and roar at them, still shocked at the violence in my own voice. My daughter stared down at me with a respectful silence: shock, perhaps, that her father—this man who played ring-around-the-rosy and let her weave dandelions into his hair—could summon such ferocity. I lifted her and instinctively inspected her for any damage; there was none. Emboldened now, I approached their new position, swinging the stick and still shouting. I threw a few more rocks, none hitting their targets. But the point was made. The dogs took off running again in the direction of the collapsing tiki huts at the abandoned zoo and disappeared.

As a kid, I dreamed of living in a city, of just walking to a corner store. I would lug my bike across a fallow cornfield to get to a gun shop, the only commercial space within many miles of my house, a windowless pole barn set on a hill overlooking the nearest blue highway, a road my father deemed too dangerous for my bike. The store was known simply as GUNS, because the word GUNS shone on its exterior in giant ten-foot letters that glowed red for miles across the county. The journey across that cornfield and back usually discouraged any follow-up visits for a few months: the ground was uneven and it was often easier just to carry the heavy Huffy than roll it through the waist-high switchgrass and forbs.

That fallow field was never replanted, as far as I know. It is currently a parking lot for a big box hardware/lumber store, with a McDonald's, a Pizza Hut, and a cell phone shop all islanded now by asphalt. This was all built after I left for college. At thirteen, it felt so liberating just to leave home on my own two wheels and go to a store, even if all it sold was weaponry I couldn't buy. I remember strolling through the aisles, staring at semiautomatics and revolvers, assault rifles and shotguns. I admired the sophisticated lines of vintage Walthers and Lugers, the slick, gimmicky plastic of Glocks, and the harsh beauty of a Sig Sauer .45 caliber handgun. I would spend hours there, dreaming of turning eighteen, examining everything from boxes of bullets to armpit holsters to compound bows and their vicious broadhead arrows. I would hover over the case of Rambo knives, listening to the clerks describe to customers what kind of damage the various pistols would do to an intruder's skull. When you're a thirteen-year-old boy, you are not just *grateful* that the only business within bike-riding distance is a gun shop and not, say, a place that sells dollhouse miniatures. You are in heaven.

One night when I was a teenager, GUNS caught fire. My father and I drove over there in his truck, while the disco lights of the local constabulary and the fire trucks and the red 10-

foot letters of GUNS itself were outmatched by the flames illuminating the night. There is a strange sense of community when some lone building in the country catches fire: neighbors come out from behind their televisions and have conversations after they might not have spoken for years; hands are shaken, news exchanged. Someone is a grandfather now. Somebody else had a good old dog die and now they got a new one. Word quickly spread throughout the township that GUNS was on fire, and soon more rubberneckers in pickup trucks were lining up along the road, all assessing the heroism of the township fire department, the performance of the brave volunteers, speculating on the possibility of some malicious cause of the blaze, and measuring the damage to our lonely island of commerce. I remember some men were drinking beer. I remember the flames reflected in eyeglasses. Before the fire was contained, the building was rocked by a series of enormous hollow, echoing explosions. "It's almost muzzle-loading season," a nearby man said. "They sell a lot of black powder there."

Then the ammo caught fire. The fire had reached it stacked up against the wall: 25-round boxes of Remington buckshot piled fifty high and ten deep, hundreds of boxes of .45 caliber bullets, and countless boxes of Winchester rifle ammunition. You could hear the bullets whistling into the darkness. The volunteer firefighters tore away from the scene in their Broncos, cops barreled toward us screaming through their loudspeakers to get the hell away from there. I've never seen my father drive so fast, my teenage body tucked snug under his right elbow, my shoulder practically against the wheel and his big battered hand around my head.

∽

My mother went back to work, like many women of her generation, after spending several years at home with my sister and me. When she did, my father quit his job teaching voc-ed car repair classes and built that shop in our backyard. When I would come home from school, Dad was always there, smelling like Bondo and primer, a splash of marina-blue acrylic basecoat cascading down his T-shirt. We would make turkey sandwiches together, watch something on television before he meandered back down to the shop, where he always seemed to be tinkering away at something he loved. I don't know if he realizes I remember all this, but I do. As I go throughout my days at home with my kid here in Detroit, I think often of my dad, how my archetypal struggle to supplant him in the end only brought me closer to him.

> *As I go throughout my days at home with my kid here in Detroit, I think often of my dad, how my archetypal struggle to supplant him in the end only brought me closer to him.*

Dad often said he would die to protect my sister and me. It was always an ominous concept in my young mind, this unalloyed testament of his love. I never had to see him prove it until that night our country home was rocked by explosions and stray bullets skimming across the fields. I doubt my daughter will remember the day I fought off the wild dogs, but down there on the ground below her I believe I was proving some kindred notion, one that is shared, perhaps, across many species. I understand what my father meant. You don't get a lot of opportunities to prove it, not even here in the second-most-dangerous city in America. But when you do, it gives you some perspective on what it means to be a father, even if you're not as tough as your old man; even when the blood on your hands comes not from your enemies, but from your own clumsy use of a simple tool. My life is nothing now if not bent toward nurturing and protecting my daughter's. I used to try to pretend that other things were as important, that parenthood would not change me or turn me into the kind of guy who spouts off these kinds of pithy truisms. But this is just the order of things. You cannot deny what comes so naturally, just like you cannot really smother wildness with cement.

James Griffioen lives with his family in Detroit, Michigan. His writing appears on the website sweet-juniper.com.

Failure

Greg Allen

The idea for the greatest short film ever came to me one Sunday afternoon while I was putting the breast pump together on the bed. The scene—the sunlight coming in the window, me standing there in my undershirt, washed and dried hardware laid out in neat rows—reminded me of the scene at the end of *The Godfather*. It was from the—SPOILER ALERT—classic massacre/baptism montage, where bloody shots of Michael Corleone's hit men simultaneously whacking five of his rival mob bosses are intercut with Corleone himself solemnly attending the baptism of his infant nephew. One assassin assembles his gun and his police uniform disguise on a hotel bed, and as a godfather, the Godfather vows to renounce evil to the swells of church organ music.

Francis Ford Coppola made *The Godfather* just as his daughter Sofia was born. By amazing coincidence, I was a filmmaker who had just become a father, too. Coppola cast his baby daughter in the baptism scene. Clearly, I would cast my own three-week-old daughter in a movie, too. And clearly, it would be a shot-for-shot remake of the climax of *The Godfather,* juxtaposing two extremes: the brutal realities of new parenthood and the carefree frivolity of kidfree life. Obviously, I would call it *The Goodfather*. And obviously, it would premiere at Sundance. The festival submission deadline was a little more than six months away. I set immediately to work.

While my wife tried to get some rest and grapple with various unexpected breastfeeding complications, I used the kid's Monday naptimes to map out the complicated structure of Coppola's montage sequence. Our daughter (out of consideration for her future Google search results, we don't publish her name) had this habit when she was awake of screaming like a banshee; it was an inescapable, piercing wail that made our Manhattan apartment feel suddenly very small, and it cleared all non-kid-comforting items from our mental to-do lists. (The kid kept this up for another ten weeks.)

> *Our daughter had this habit when she was awake of screaming like a banshee; it was an inescapable, piercing wail that made our Manhattan apartment feel suddenly very small, and it cleared all non-kid-comforting items from our mental to-do lists.*

With a storyboard in place and a screaming baby rehearsing her lines day and night, I thought it best to get the scenes of wild, partying abandon in the can first. I would take my DV camera to the Museum of Modern Art Film Department fund-raising gala I was cohosting the next day. The honoree's latest film was up for several Academy Awards, and most of the stars she'd worked with were expected to attend. The film was *Lost in Translation,* and the director was Sofia Coppola. It was barely March; if the banshee cooperated, maybe I could even edit the movie together in time for the Venice film festival in August. Or at least Toronto in September.

Around lunchtime Tuesday, I lost my assistant camera operator. My wife decided that no, two weeks after giving birth and facing another bout of mastitis, she did not, in fact, feel like attending a celebrity party at MoMA, especially one that involved tooling around with a video camera all night, and I should plan on going by myself. I folded my storyboard into one suit pocket and my introductory speech into the other.

As soon as I got to the old Gramercy Theater, where the first half of the MoMA event was being held, I realized it wouldn't be easy to actually match Coppola's original shots; I'd have to do some creative homage. Instead of a massage table, I'd shoot the bar. Instead of imposing courthouse steps, the street and the theater marquee. Instead of a revolving hotel door, the red carpet. It's better not to be too literal anyway; the intercutting and the family connection would be insidery and amusing enough to carry it.

There was no one really at the bar, but I got nice shots of rows of cans of Sofia champagne from the Coppola family winery. Kirsten Dunst and her boyfriend pulled up in a big black Escalade as I was shooting the marquee. Then Sofia herself arrived in a poofy white Marc Jacobs dress and milled about on the red carpet for a while. This was going to be great. I went in to check my seat. Quentin Tarantino wandered into my aisle; he was sitting next to me. We chatted, I explained my project. He loved it! Sofia and her producer came up; we chatted for a few minutes. The program was getting ready to start. I grabbed a couple more shots of people drinking cans of Sofia. Just as the lights were dimming, the

New Yorker writer Lillian Ross slid in and sat in what had been my wife's seat. She was like a super-nice, super-literary grandma. We chatted about my little film project. "Congratulations!" she said, when I told her who I'd gotten to play the kid.

My thank-you speech is three thank-you speeches in, I turn to Quentin—I feel like I can call him Quentin now—and ask if he'll shoot my speech for me. He smirks a "no way" smirk and but just says, "Dude." (Wait, I thought he loved my project?) I end up taking the video camera with me, filming as I go. As I cross in front of the crowd, I stop and do a pan. Scattered laughter. Then I see Bill Murray is sitting right next to the podium. Impulsively, I hand him my camera, still rolling, and asked if he'll shoot me for a little movie I'm making—desperate times, desperate measures, I have to say it—for my new daughter, who is home with my wife.

My cohost and co-thanker is a downtown art collector named Hillary; she's been dressed by a sponsor. About thirty seconds into our speech, Bill hops up from his seat and starts walking around us. People laugh. I introduce my assistant camera operator, ladies and gentlemen, Mr. Bill Murray. Slightly baffled applause. Murray starts panning up and down Hillary's gown, asking who it's by, and then he zooms in on her cleavage. The audience roars. Not sure how I'll work that footage into the movie, though. Definitely something breastfeeding-related. We finish our thank-yous to great applause. Back at my seat, Quentin congratulates me. Jimmy Fallon turns around to tell me we killed.

At the after-party, I quickly run out of tape shooting impressionistic B-roll of the buffet and the dance floor. I retire to the VIP room, where Quentin, Jim Jarmusch, and I talk seriously about Gus Van Sant's shot-for-shot remake of *Psycho*. I warn a very pregnant Marcia Gay Harden and her husband off from the Diaper Genie. As Fallon and friends finally make ready to leave, I head out, too. On the way, I thank Bill and joke about the lameness of benefit speeches. Then the man from freakin' *Caddyshack* goes, "Well, I thought you were very funny." I'm so high on myself, I can't remember what else we talked about; I think he said he has ten kids. On the way home, I decide, as a courtesy, I should contact Murray's agent before upgrading him to director of photography. Wouldn't want any awkwardness at the *Goodfather* premiere party.

The next morning, I find out my wife's mastitis had gotten so painful, she had her sister take her to the emergency room. I don't recap the party for her. Two weeks went by—two rough weeks, where the kid was practicing her lines, this time with *feeling,* and where we could barely hold it together through the day or night—before I even got a chance to screen the party footage. It was all I could do to burn Bill's speech scene onto a few DVDs and pass them around. Truly hilarious, though; this is going to be great.

As for the kid, yes, I needed shots of screaming, but most of the time, what I really needed was to get the screaming to stop. As long as I get it in the can before my wife heads back to work, I figured, I'd be fine. Weeks churn by, and I don't make it. Now on my own with the kid during the day—rather than hire a nanny, the classic uptown approach, I'd decided to take a few months off and then work from home—I really find out taking care of a newborn is plenty of work even without trying to make a movie of the whole process.

The real snag was that I couldn't bring myself to try. When-

ever the kid went on a crying jag, I had to, wanted to calm her
down. By the end of May, the deadline for Venice missed, the
film was in serious trouble. Not only had the kid completely
outgrown her wrinkly, newborn Sofia-at-baptism look, she'd
cut down dramatically on the crying. In fact, she'd actually
mellowed right out. If I wanted her to cry now, I'd have to
make her cry. And I just couldn't. My perfectly conceived, perfectly half-shot film was in danger of—come on, who was I
fooling? It was blown. Over. There was no way around it: my
daughter wasn't getting a film in Sundance before her first
birthday, and it was all my fault.

Here I was, trying like generations of dads before me, to properly express my paternal love through projects—inordinately
elaborate stuff-making, ideally requiring a large workshop full
of expensive and esoteric tools—and I'd failed miserably on
the very first try. Sure, I'd painted the nursery and assembled
the crib, but those were merely the ante in the great Texas
hold'em of fatherhood. I know a guy who actually enlisted in
Rocking Chair University in order to get one of those sleek,
Sam Maloof–style, heirloom rockers finished before his kid arrived. Dad mags from the fifties were stuffed with all kinds of
blueprints for making things for the kids: a toy box shaped like
your battleship from the Korean War; a Willy's Jeep cut and
welded from the sheet metal lying around the garage; a handy
TV-watching bench made from those old paint cans you were
going to throw away. My own dad had even built me a 4-foot-
wide cardboard and Mylar parabolic mirror for a third-grade
science project.

Living in the city, with no workbench and only the basic
tools, I was already at a disadvantage. But even using the tools I

DID have, my DV cameras and digital editing software, I'd failed. It didn't bode well. *The Goodfather* turned out to be only the first in a string of dad project failures that haunt my first three years as a parent.

My next big failure, the Mini-boo, was of this "for the want of a workshop" variety, though if we'd actually lived in the suburbs, it would have never come up in the first place. Our playground in Central Park has a particularly fierce toy stroller culture. Lots of kids bring them, and lots of kids obsess over, play with, and fight for them. When my daughter was eighteen months old, the kid was thoroughly caught up in the frenzy. She wanted her own rig, and I wanted to get her one, if only to avoid the stigma of being labeled a perennial playground mooch.

The problem was, most toy strollers are umbrella-style models, and we had a Bugaboo. Though the kid would merrily grab on to whatever toy stroller was in reach, I worried about the unforeseen developmental and bonding problems that might arise if the kid's toy stroller didn't match her real stroller. Also, who wants a toy stroller like everyone else's? No, I knew the kid should have a toy Bugaboo—a Mini-boo—and if there wasn't one on the market, I'd make it myself.

I mulled the Mini-boo over all summer and into the fall. As she became aware of the whole Christmas gift concept, the only thing the kid wanted from Santa was a stroller. This was not a drill. I spotted an aluminum and nylon picnic basket from Germany that looked remarkably like a Bugaboo. It's already 80 percent of the way there, I figured. Just stick some wheels on there, and I'll be done: instant Mini-boo. I could probably even make it on the kitchen table.

As I designed and built it in my head, I came to realize how the Mini-boo would play a formative role in my daughter's memories of her childhood. Long after the playground crowds dispersed, the Mini-boo would become a cherished heirloom, an extraordinary souvenir of her first celebration of Christmas. It was her Rosebud. Or it would be, as soon as Santa got around to actually building the thing.

The picnic basket only came out at night, after the kid was asleep, and my wife and I would puzzle over it. She figured out how to invert half the basket to make the seat. Looking Bugaboo-ish was important, but it also had to work as a toy. The major challenge would be getting the handle height and angle right, so an almost-two-year-old could push it. Which meant sticking a couple of wheels on the bottom of the basket wouldn't work; I'd have to build a little chassis like on the real Bugaboo. And with no fabrication capacity, I'd have to build it from scavenged and repurposed material with little more than a Dremel, a power drill, and my new pop riveter.

Home Depot was useless, but combing thrift shops turned up some sweet aluminum crutches I could take apart. When training wheels didn't work, I found some nice, big rubber wheels and aluminum tubing at a model airplane store down-town. Assembly took a few sporadic nights in December. Dremel-on-aluminum made an unbearable, grinding whine, so I had to move the project down to the laundry room, which closed at 10 P.M. Designing as I went helped reduce the project to a series of discrete problems to be solved. But the compro-mises I had to make at each step were a little disheartening. I had a platonic ideal of a Mini-boo in my head, but as it gradually took shape, my little Franken-boo was turning out different. Still, it was done in time, and it rolled, and damned if it didn't look quite a bit like a Bugaboo.

When Christmas morning came, the kid got high just shredding wrapping paper. We opened gifts from the grandparents and such before getting to Santa's and Daddy's present. (I took partial credit in order to explain to the kid why I'd need to be tweaking her Mini-boo for the first few weeks. Turns out Christmas was not the end of the project, but the first round of user testing.) The stroller was perfect. The kid was thrilled. She put her pig in and started pushing her around the house while I hovered, my nervous eyes watching the epoxied joints.

I spent the rest of winter tinkering with the axles, which were very wobbly. They needed something to counter the splaying pressure the kid'd put on the rig when she leaned into it and pushed. In mid-March, still wearing our jackets, we headed out to the playground one sunny afternoon to dazzle the world with the Mini-boo. The kid pushed the stroller along the sidewalk for a while, but the wobbly wheels made me nervous, so I told her it was best to carry it to the playground instead. We entered the park by Tavern on the Green, walked up the hill to the playground, closed the gate, and set the Mini-boo on the foamy playmat surface. The kid toddled forward with it about ten feet, and I glanced around to see if anyone recognized the greatness of my creation. Suddenly, a reaction: a boy maybe two, two-and-a-half, spotted the Mini-boo, headed toward it in a dead run, ran into it, and squashed it flat. Every epoxied joint snapped, and the struts all fell apart and rolled around. A nervous nanny offered a singsongy apology to the air as she helped her charge flee the scene of the crime.

After an initial flurry of Mini-boo requests, the stroller was eventually pushed out of sight. It migrated to the top of the front closet, then the top of our bedroom closet. When the kid started attending a little preschool, her playground habits changed, and toy strollers were suddenly for little kids. Now if she mentions it at all, the Mini-boo is not Christmas or the indoor euphoria of those first, wintry months; it's the stroller that deadbeat Santa was too busy to fix. And for me, of course, it'll always be the toy—the overambitious and underengineered improvisation of a toy—that I couldn't make for my kid.

My third dad-project failure is ongoing. For years, even before having a kid, I had a mind to make a crib in the severe, minimalist style of the sculptor Donald Judd. For his SoHo loft, Judd had made a giant daybed by surrounding a double mattress on three sides with imposing slabs of inch-thick fir, which would make a killer crib. Unfortunately, Judd—who passed away in 1996—had not designed a toddler-sized version, so I'd have to figure it out myself. A couple of estimates came back around five thousand dollars; apparently, they don't make inch-thick slabs of fir like they used to. The decision point was coming, though; the kid was outgrowing her crib, and would soon need a toddler bed of some kind. John, an artist friend in Brooklyn with access to a CNC router, offered to help, and over the course of about three months, we began designing and making a scaled-down crib inspired by Judd's daybed out of clear birch plywood.

Unimaginable engineering problems drew out the process

to absurd lengths. Because there were no certified inspections for the one-off crib, the design had to be blindingly obviously safe. The assembled bed wouldn't fit through the kid's bedroom door, so we couldn't just glue it together. It had to come apart, but to be true to Judd's spirit, I insisted the pristine geometric form could not be marred by visible hardware. So the wood shop guys and I spent weeks ordering, trying, and then discarding various embedded, invisible joinery technologies. (Months after we found our esoteric and expensive hardware solution, John and I attended a Judd exhibition and saw the many, many different types of totally visible screws and bolts the artist used over the years.)

As the months and man-hours and machine-hours and hardware experiments ticked by, the tab on the $500–$700 crib passed $2,500, and that's not counting the sweet safety rail, made out of thick, round-edged, molded Plexiglas by the Plexiglas guy upstate, or the organic toddler futon the kid used on the floor as she waited for her bed, which she outgrew before the bed was finished. And it doesn't include the cost of designing and fabricating a crib front. Because in the meantime, we are expecting a second kid. And I have only a few months to finish what will be the sweetest, most minimalist crib ever. Can't wait to see how that turns out.

Greg Allen is a former private equity consultant turned writer and filmmaker. His Souvenir Series of short documentaries about memory has screened at film festivals and the Museum of Modern Art, and he is adapting a screenplay from a nineteenth-century Icelandic novel. He writes for The New York Times *on film, video art, and art collect-*

ing, and has also reviewed strollers for Slate. *Before his first daughter was born in 2004, Allen launched Daddy Types: the weblog for new dads. He lives in New York City and Washington, D.C., where his wife works as an astrophysicist at NASA, and where his daughter learns the difference between "train," "subway," and "Metro."*

Peas and Domestic Tranquility

Greg Knauss

The first conscious parental thought I ever had—cradling my bawling three-week-old son in my arms and staring out the window at the gray light crawling over the horizon—was, "Okay. Don't kill the baby."

The previous weeks had been packed with various adoring *unconscious* parental thoughts, coming in unexpected and up-ending waves: So *this* is what pure love is; I have the most amazing wife in the whole world; he smiled, I swear he smiled, not gas, it was a smile, at *me*; good God, is that *tar* coming out of his ass?

But this was a very intentional and seriously considered conscious thought, something I had very intentionally and seriously worked at, very intentionally and seriously forced into my head. It was required in the face of the new and ugly unconscious thoughts that were suddenly welling up from some dark corner of my sanity after a series of long and grindingly slow nights spent cajoling, begging, and ultimately attempting to bribe the boy to just goddamned go to *sleep,* sweet holy Christ, just please go to *sleep.*

Okay. Don't kill the baby. Breathe in, breathe out. No baby killing. Okay.

Raising a child is easily the most maddening thing I've ever done. It is, of course, also the most rewarding thing I've ever done. The latter gets a lot of attention—frozen in time and assembled neatly in picture albums, scrapbooks, family stories—while the former, nearly as significant in the big, day-to-day scheme of things, is the subject of only ominous public service announcements and scolding looks from strangers, your parents, and your mate. Everybody gets mad at their kids; nobody likes to talk about it.

You bring an infant home from the hospital, and he seems the smallest, most delicate, most beautiful thing you've ever seen in your life. He's brand new, a brand new person, and you are there to protect him and nurture him and teach him and mold him and help him to become the man who is everything that he might be. And he grows! He grows so fast. And he acquires a personality, and a will of his own, and he has wants and needs and he matures and blossoms in ways that you wouldn't have dreamt of those first few special weeks. And as much as you love him and cherish him and are proud of him, you simply cannot freakin' goddamned *believe* the massive trail of destruction he's left in his wake. God! Just once, please just once, will you clean up your room? *God!*

Do *not* kill the baby.

This cocktail of deep love and rattling frustration defines fatherhood for me, especially now that I have three boys and they're all old enough to enrage me, both individually or working as a team, like wolves. Tom is eight, Mike seven, and Pete six.

They're all smart, alas, and this manifests itself in an almost lawyer-like ability to intentionally misconstrue or narrowly interpret anything I say. They each take a special delight in proving their cleverness and/or my stupidity by hammering every hot button that they've found in my psyche like it was a Whac-A-Mole. It's their job, of course, driving Dad crazy. My job is to correct any impression they have that the entire world revolves around them, that whatever whim is driving them at the moment might not be as important as the larger goals that we, as a family and a society, are working toward.

They're better at their job than I am at mine, a lot of the time.

Part of the problem is that they're boys, and do as boys do. There's something genetic about it, something in the combination of cultural conditioning and a penis that breeds a strong desire to see your brother sent to his room, even if you have to follow him there. "Boys will be boys" isn't so much an excuse for the behavior as a prediction of it.

A couple of years ago, we spent an afternoon at the park with some friends and their three girls. While the girls sat in the sand and shared toys and bonded in a way that was only missing a few glasses of wine or some chocolate ice cream, my sons ran in noisy circles around them, trying to punch each other in the face. "Wow," my friend said. "Is that what boys are like?"

"Yeah."

"Man. They just . . . Wow."

"If it makes you feel any better for me, your kids are going to mutate into teenage girls at some point, and that will make this little melee look like tea with the Queen. The boys are just going to keep hitting each other. The only thing I have to worry about is fratricide. Your girls are going to run psy-ops campaigns that would make the CIA curl into a fetal ball and cry itself to sleep."

"Uh . . ."

"Ha, ha-ha, ha."

You take your victories where you can find them. My friend and I are boys, too.

Another problem is that we're outnumbered, my wife and I. Since Peter was born, we've had to play zone defense instead of man-to-man, and the stats show it.

Remember those maze games, where you tilt the board to maneuver a marble along a path, avoiding each hole until you got to the end? Having three boys is like that, but with three marbles, and they're all sentient, and they goddamned well don't *want* to get to the end, and if you pick one up and deposit it into its hole, it's only going to climb right out while you chase down the other two. I used to shout at the game, too.

> *Remember those maze games, where you tilt the board to maneuver a marble along a path, avoiding each hole until you got to the end? Having three boys is like that.*

Or here: There's a scene in the first *Jurassic Park* movie, where two velociraptors distract a smarter and better-armed dinosaur hunter, so that a third—sharp-eyed and with a mouthful of daggers—can sneak up on him from the side and leave his intestines piled up at his feet. That's what our house is like.

And finally, and unfortunately, raising children is only part of my life—an important part, of course, but it can only consume some significant fraction of my time and attention. The house must be kept from actually collapsing in on itself. Employment must be tended to in some convincing way. Hygiene and sleep play small roles. Cars break down, toilets blow up, investments fall apart, illnesses and crises and even the occasional good thing happen, and always life goes on. Each and every one of these things consumes patience, time, and whatever tattered remains of my sanity have made it to this point. Children can simply be the maddening, disobedient cherry on top of the ice cream sundae of modern, postmillennial life. If Daddy comes home from work with his unhappy face—you know, the red one, with the teeth bared and the tendons in his neck all tight like that—it should merely be survival instinct not to have a screaming contest. But no. The screaming contest must be had.

But aside from all the contributing factors—their gender, their number, all the other things that contribute to the impending sense of disaster that hangs over any house with young children—what ultimately defines the scope, shape, and magnitude of paternal anger is what the kids themselves do, and how I react to it. I can offer all the mitigation and explanation in the world, and what it comes down to is me and them.

The ugly shame of it is that I'm not the perfect father, and as much as I love my kids, they are not the perfect sons. We struggle sometimes, as does every family. Anger—theirs, mine, my wife's, the dog's—is part of life. It's not all of it, of course, and some happy, too-rare days it doesn't even feel like the majority of it. But if you accept the fact that it's there, and that you're going to have to deal with it, and fight it, and maybe—just maybe, a little at a time—best it, you have to be able to identify it.

Here's what I've found that sets me off: disobedience, lying, and rudeness. Each is a form of the previous, building and adding nuance, and each can drive me completely stark-raving bonkers. Depending on the circumstances, they earn anything from a sit-com-level whadda-ya-gonna-do shrug to a red-faced, where's-the-knives rage.

Everybody's list will be different. My children are not cruel—at least not to anybody they're not related to—nor greedy nor lazy. They have vast reservoirs of kindness in them, even generosity, and they love with a sweetness and purity that I can't even *begin* to understand. But this is the real world, and we clash, again and again and again. The point is to move toward something, some victory, some stalemate, some truce that both sides can live with, some peace.

We're not there yet.

Children need to have firm boundaries set. They need to know the rules. They actually seek out these stable environments, the books and psychologists and experts say, quoting each other. The child-rearing-advice industry burps up this aphorism with a steady, rhythmic thump, like sausages being pumped out of a machine.

But my theory goes that children seek order only so they have an opportunity to disrupt it, to abuse it, to take it out back and kick it in the teeth until it sobs. Chaos amid chaos is no fun. Chaos at dinner is a ball.

Disobedience is the single most frustrating thing my kids do, the easiest way to spark my anger. I'm not a tyrant or a bully—not much anyway—but I am a father and I expect to be minded when I say that punting a football is an outside activity. To be willfully ignored, defied, *laughed off* by children told explicitly what to do or not do is a tunnel straight into every anxiety I have about my own powerlessness. It would say more about me than about them if they didn't revel in it so much.

Take dinner. It's a pretty simple thing: You sit down, you eat, you clean up. Easy. But every dinner we've had for the past half-decade has ultimately reduced down to a battle between the forces of good (me) and evil (them). This is my essay and I get to say who the hero is.

Sit. Eat. Speak quietly. Sit. No throwing. Sit. No mocking. Don't tease. Eat. Sit. I said no throwing! Especially peas!

I emphasize sitting because it seems to be the simplest element of this very simple activity. That it's not only a point of contention but also a serious one, does not auger well for the rest of the meal, or night, or adolescence. I don't know where the drive to stand up during dinner comes from, but given that all three boys are compelled to do it every minute of every meal we've ever eaten together, I'm guessing that the answer is Hell. On bad nights, after bad days, their inability to just goddamned *sit down,* after suggestions raised to demands raised to orders raised to threats, has driven me upstairs to shake in private fury.

This is what saying "Sit in your chair properly" looks like when it's said a hundred times, over the course of twenty minutes:

Sit in your chair properly. Sit in your chair properly. Sit in your chair properly! In your chair; I'm not telling you again. In. Your. Chair. Now. Look, okay, both legs in front, tush all the way back. Simple. Okay? OKAY. SIT IN YOUR CHAIR! That's it! I've had it! Sit! Chair! DON'T THROW PEAS!

I've never actually made it to a hundred. I just tell them that I have, later. It seems the classic parental repetition number.

Is this boundary-testing? Is this bored dismissiveness? Is this a devious plan to trigger a massive coronary and collect the insurance? Do they simply think that it's funny watching Dad push the stone up the hill every night, just to watch it roll down again?

I've been tempted to think of it as pathological, that there's something diseased in them that needs America's pharmacological best—a good-sized horse pill that will drug them into a compliant torpor. And then I think that I'd much rather have the pill for myself. And then I end up just sending them to their room, where they can fall asleep, forget that they're missing dessert, and dream of plans for the next night's fun.

Disobedience is an omnipresent part of parenthood. In my calmer moments, I realize it's an essential part of growing up, of discovering that what you want can be independent of what the powers-that-be want, and if you're strong and persistent and willing to bear punishment for your insolence, you may just get your way. I spent too much of my childhood (and adolescence and adulthood) in unquestioning fealty to whoever or whatever happened to be in front of me, demanding compliance—my parents, my teachers, my friends. Decades later, I still feel the resentment of perpetually doing what I was told. I had a hard time learning to speak up for myself, to take a stand in defiance of someone claiming authority. When Tom was born, I swore that that particular personality defect wasn't going to be his—my boys would be fair and kind, but nobody's pushover. They would have the self-confidence to decide on a course, stake out a position, and defend it, without apology. I looked forward to the day that one of my sons, defiance in his eyes, stood before me and said, "No, Dad. You're wrong. Screw you!"

I had just thought that it would be at sixteen, not six.

I'm getting what I deserve, of course. The grim satisfaction that your grandparents felt when your parents complained about how much trouble you were is now your parents' to enjoy. I was obedient—too obedient—but I managed to do my parent-frustrating in other ways: I was coward enough to lie.

Twenty-five years ago, I had closed my door and dumped out the plastic bag on my bed and laid out the salvaged fireworks like any good borderline-autistic would: by class, then color, then fuse length. Most of the survivors I'd scavenged off the beach the day after the Fourth of July had been lit, tossed, and then fizzled in the sand. One in particular—a small firecracker with a blue-and-white pattern—had the merest nub of fuse left, poking out the top.

I picked up one of the discarded lighters lying next to the fireworks and—with all the forethought and common sense of a fourteen-year-old—tried to see how close I could get the flame to that fuse without actually lighting it.

In retrospect, this strikes me as perhaps not the best idea.

The firecracker went off in my hand with an explosion that seemed like it sucked the air into the space where the firecracker used to be, before blowing it out again, smoke and little bits of paper debris and my very surprised shout suddenly appearing from nowhere.

I don't know how long it took—time passes slowly when you're trying to keep your urine in—but the door to my room banged open and my mom lunged in and said, "What was *that*?"

And I stood up and turned around—lighter still in my hand, smoke and firecracker confetti drifting down around me and the faintest echo of a loud bang still bouncing around the room—and said: "I don't know!"

You may notice the lie. Come a certain age, children learn that they can lie, but they're not very good at it. The skill that some will acquire as adults in law school or real estate seminars or marriage counseling hasn't blossomed yet and they're left with the simple calculus of: I've just done something that I don't want to admit to. Ergo, I won't. Easy!

I honestly don't remember my mom's response to that, but I do remember that even to my tiny, responsibility-free brain, it seemed a feeble answer. So I elaborated: "It must have been smoldering! And, and, and just went off now!" I had the lighter in my hand, remember.

This is a lie upon a lie, the start of an endless spiral that will end with a child denying your paternity simply to get out of brushing his teeth. The danger is that lying will become habit, become a matter of course. When they get good at it—when they can build lies out of something other than gossamer and wishes—the lack of any sort of guilt about it will unleash on the world a monster, a villain, a politician.

"Did you clean your room?"

"Yes."

"But it's not clean. Look. There're clothes all over the floor. And it looks like something is nesting in your closet."

"But I cleaned it!"

"Then how do you explain the fact that it's not clean?"

"Why do you hate America?"

And for all my righteous anger about the lies themselves, perhaps more maddening is the implicit assumption behind them: My father is an idiot. Lying is a different face of disobedience, a sneakier one. It relies not on defiance, but on subterfuge. I would much rather one of my sons continue to kick a ball against the side of the house—dropping acoustical cottage cheese in clumps and rattling knickknacks off the mantel—in violation of my strict instructions of twenty seconds ago, than to do it and then deny that it was him.

If anything crystallizes the Pyrrhic victories of fatherhood, it's the fact that my fondest wish is for hooligans instead of sociopaths. I think the lying bothers me so much not because they're trying to get away with anything—though the sneaky little bastards certainly are—but because I see my own weaknesses and failures in it. Lying is about not having the confidence to defend what you've done. Lying is about weaseling out of the consequences of your actions. I was a liar because it seemed easier.

I get angry at my kids for lying because now I know it's not.

One thing that I used to believe that *has* stuck with me is, of course, that farts are funny. Burps, too. Sneezes, even. Pretty much the whole gamut of bodily noises is a treasure trove of ready-made comedy. You gather a handful of small boys together and let them entertain themselves and there will be more sharp honks than an angry L.A. freeway. But there's a time and place for such fun, and every second of every day, no matter the location or company, turns out not to be the appropriate venue for a gastrointestinal symphony.

My sons will sit at the dinner table—the dinner table, again—and tilt their heads back and open their mouths like young birds, waiting to be fed. And the windows will rattle in their frames. Forks will clatter to plates and appalled looks will be made and the trumpeter will look put-upon and claim, "I couldn't stop it!" Which isn't disobedience or a lie so much as it is the simple selfishness, a dismissal of the sensibilities of others. I felt like cutting loose, so I cut loose. And it was funny as *hell*.

The anger at this point is usually my wife's and it's usually directed at me, since, yeah, he's got a point.

No, no! Wait! I mean, that's rude! That's awful! Where did you learn your manners, young man?

And I end up shouting at them, just to be heard over the laughing.

Years ago, before my kids were born, I was the weird uncle

to a couple of rowdy nephews, and I was struck by how polite they were. They always said "Please" and they always said "Thank you" and they seemed to genuinely mean it. It wasn't just the fact that they'd been trained into our modern social conventions, but that they knew the meaning behind the kabuki: I am asking you for something, something you don't necessarily have to give me. So I'll be polite.

I swore that my kids would do the same. How hard can it be, teaching basic respect to small, open minds? How hard can it be for someone to learn to be grateful for something that they might not have otherwise gotten? How many times can I be so profoundly, deeply, totally wrong?

"Give me ice cream."

"Excuse me?"

"Give me ice cream."

"Let's try that again."

"I said, give me ice cream."

"That's rude."

"So is not giving me ice cream."

"I'm waiting for the magic word."

"Now."

"Oh, here, look. We have some ice cream. And it's spanking flavored!"

If disobedience is maddening because it's active and open defiance, and lying is maddening because it's sneaky and covert dismissal, then rudeness is maddening because it's thoughtless and self-satisfied arrogance. Oh, were you there? How about that? You don't like having your dinner interrupted with an air horn? Huh. How, exactly, does that affect me?

The rules are simple: The floor is not where dirty clothes

are stored; a telephone has a person on the other end, so when someone is talking into one, it counts as a conversation; the bathroom has a door for a freakin' reason; and your need for a snack, no matter how desperate, can probably wait another two minutes.

They're not spoiled, or at least that's what they insist while listing the various foods, electronic devices, and weapons they are denied. They have the capacity for empathy, and it pokes its head out in the most unexpected and wonderful ways. But too often and too vehemently, they claim their place by pushing others aside.

Written down, it seems a small thing, to be polite. But the implications are perhaps more important than anything else I can teach them. On a larger scale, rudeness is a fundamental disregard for the fact that there are other people in the world, and they may have some claim on whatever it is you happen to want at the moment—everything is not exclusively about you.

This idea doesn't come preinstalled in children, and must be pounded in, sometimes with a mallet. Respect—for themselves and for others—is the foundation for nothing less than how we should treat each other. Politeness is the first step toward that, rudeness the first step in the other direction.

And if I have to shout to make them understand that, well then, it's a good thing they don't recognize hypocrisy yet.

Disobedience, lying, rudeness. It's not a bad list—none of them are felonies—and they *are* good kids. They're wonderful kids. But faced with the restless, relentless energy of my boys, how they apply it, and the slow grinding crush of modern life, anger can sprout and split and multiply and *emerge*, fully formed, out of nowhere—unwelcome and unbidden, but here, now. It's something that every parent deals with, some better than others.

And so, I get angry. Too often and too deeply, I get angry. Sometimes, bad times, it seems like all I do. It's weakness and exhaustion and frustration, it's fear of what may be and sadness for what is, it's everything I don't want to be and everything I can't control.

But I love my sons, with all the ferocity that my heart can muster. They are my life, and the family that we have built— my boys, my wife, and I—is the single most important thing I have ever done, or ever will do. It's not perfect—it lurches and falters, like any family—and I am not even close to its perfect shepherd. But as my boys grow—so fast, so terrifyingly fast— maybe they will see their father more deeply than he can show himself, and take my true meaning from what I have damned through my anger. Maybe they will grow to be men better than I am, men who can—

I SAID STOP THROWING PEAS! *DAMMIT!*

Greg Knauss lives in Los Angeles with his wife, three boys, his dog, and a mortgage. His website is www.eod.com.

Part Three

AFTER THE WAR

My Father Makes Sense, and Other Harsh Realities of Adulthood

Heather B. Armstrong

The phone rings, and when I answer it, I hear my father's gloomy Southern voice on the other end.

"Feather," he says, calling me by the nickname I've had since birth. "This is your dad."

Up until a year ago, before he moved to a home near us in Utah, he would always greet me and my husband on the phone with, "It's Mike from Tennessee," as if we wouldn't recognize his distinct voice, or as if there were so many other Mikes in our life that he needed to specify "the one from Tennessee." This is just one of an endless number of reasons why my father is the most civilized person on the planet, that even when making chitchat with his own daughter, he goes out of his way to make sure everyone is on an even playing field: "Hello! Before we begin our discussion, let me give you a brief biography of the person on this end of the line so that you may be adequately prepared to navigate the next three minutes of your life!"

"Hey, Dad," I say. "How are you?"

"I'm okay. Listen, I need to talk to you. Do you have a second?"

I've been lying horizontally on the couch, but when I hear him say "need," I sit upright. My father rarely needs anything, and he doesn't ever call me and use this tone of voice, one of worry and uncertainty. I've probably only heard this particular tone in his voice twice in my life, once when I was ten and he was in the middle of a divorce with my mother. Oddly, I don't have many bad memories of that time in my life, probably because my parents couldn't have handled it better, but I do remember many mornings spent sitting with my father in his empty bedroom listening to Air Supply records. That band has become to our whole family the mascot for our parents' divorce, and even now when I hear one of their songs, I expect someone in the room to be crying, either from heartbreak or because their ears are bleeding.

The only other time I have heard this unsettled tone in my father's voice was in my early twenties when I was feeling foolishly bold during a friendly phone call and offhandedly said, "If I were Bill Clinton, I'd have lied about it, too!" That was the first of several times that my father disowned me.

Usually when he calls, he's beaming at having just saved 40 cents on a loaf of bread, and the purpose of our conversation is to celebrate that victory. Almost every sentence that comes out of his mouth includes a word or two about the importance of being frugal. It is the guiding force of his life, one that when coupled with an unparalleled work ethic, enabled him to escape the destitute trappings of his youth, a time in his life when his family rarely knew how they'd afford the next meal. And now, even though he sits on a mountain of money that he has saved throughout his life, he still won't buy anything without a coupon. Sometimes this can be charming, like here is this cute, balding rich man who has been wearing the same pair of tennis shoes for nine years. He's still so genuine, so *real*. But more often than not, it is infuriating because he cannot let it go, is unable to let us buy him dinner because a meal that someone paid full price for would make his teeth fall out.

The month after he moved to Utah, he frantically phoned me to try and figure out what was going on with the taxes people in this state have to pay on various utility bills. The fact that Utah law prevents him from consolidating his bills, that he must consequently pay taxes ON EVERY SINGLE BILL, was reason enough to blame the state when he died of heart failure. The thought that he'd be giving all those extra pennies to the government every month, it incensed him because *he wanted to be buried with those pennies*. The bright side, I told him, was that his coffin, it would be lighter!

I tease my father that he should wear a medical tag around his neck so that if anyone ever finds his body in the woods, they'd know what killed him. His father wore one for diabetes. My father's tag should read: MISERLY.

I don't know if it's in my DNA to approach money the same way or if it's something he hammered mercilessly into my upbringing, but sadly, I, too, have a hard time parting with any portion of my paycheck and instead like to pack it away into my jowls like a maniacal chipmunk in a race against the seasons. In my early twenties while working in Los Angeles for an Internet start-up, I bought a new car and financed it on a two-year payment plan, a stunningly daring impulse on par with BASE jumping from the top of my two-story apartment building. The idea of carrying around debt a second longer than I needed to made me sicker to my stomach than the fact that my car payment would cost more than my rent. And when I paid it off two years later, having not missed a single payment, my credit score shot through the roof. Suddenly, at the young age of twenty-five, I started receiving letters from banks and credit card companies with offers of credit lines up to $100,000, a fact that made my father as proud as if he were the one who had taught Michael Jordan how to dribble.

That was the first time in my life that I realized just how much I resembled my father, and not just physically. I had always known that the majority of my features had been determined by the X chromosome he'd given me, how my legs started at my ears, how the only curve in my silhouette was the jarring line of my pointy chin, how my metabolism could melt steel from across the room. But I always thought that the rest of me—my studiousness, my anxiety, the way I write a poem—all those other things were mirror images of my mother. And when I bought that car, when I looked at all my options and made my own decision as to what I thought was best, I suddenly realized that I agreed with my father. Holy crap! *I got his brain, too.*

Most of my memories of my father are colored with his relentless need to be frugal, but the most vivid ones I have are of him dressed in the suits he wore to his office job, one he worked for over thirty-five years. They were dark, always pressed into long creases, and at night after work when he changed into more comfortable clothing, I always noticed the hairless patches of skin on his knees and ankles, the places on his body rubbed raw from the constant friction of moving around in his suits. He did not do the physical work of a farmer or construction worker, but I understood that those hidden patches on his body were as symbolic as a calloused finger or hand. You could look at his knees and see the years of his life he sacrificed to make ends meet.

I also remember him being very playful, wrestling me and my siblings on the living room floor, talking to us in cartoon voices, and playing us records by the Bee Gees. In fact, my father made sure that I was acquainted with Barry, Robin, and Maurice Gibb before I came out of the womb. They were the only records my father owned, plus a couple less important ones by ABBA and Anne Murray. And while it would have been so much cooler had I grown up listening to the Stones or Zeppelin or anything featuring men who don't sing like women, I can't say that I have any hard feelings about my Bee Gees upbringing, or the consequent 25-year crush I've had on skinny, bearded men.

My father's favorite Bee Gees song was "Nights on Broadway," and he used to set the needle specifically to that point in the record to serenade his Saturday afternoon chores. I can remember those afternoons distinctly, because I *loved* it when he blamed it all on the nights on Broadway, and because he usually did his chores dressed in nothing but plaid shorts, an old white T-shirt, and a pair of mid-calf black socks. My favorite part was when he'd drop whatever he was doing as the song got to the chorus, scrunch his forehead like he had been kicked in the groin, and scream, "BLAMING IT ALL!" For years I couldn't imagine the enormity of what must have happened on Broadway, something scandalous for sure, because they were blaming everything on that one road. And I couldn't wait until I could grow up and blame it ALL on Broadway, too.

All these memories are of a man who never uses such a concerned tone of voice, at least not loosely. I can't imagine why he's calling me like this, so I decide to continue our conversation carefully.

"What's going on?" I ask, a little afraid.

"Well," he begins, "can I ask you something?"

"Of course," I say.

"Does your husband like us?" he asks.

I want to tell him immediately that, of course, my husband Jon loves him. Jon loves all of my family despite the fact that they conduct themselves in a manner that suggests it is their God-given right to park a pickup truck on *your* front lawn. But before I answer, I'm struck dumb with the implications of such a question. What happened between Jon and my father? When? Jon understands explicitly that he is never supposed to bring up something potentially upsetting when in the company of my family, something like religion or politics or feminine hygiene, because one, it will only end up in a useless argument, and two, my father owns a gun.

A few weeks ago we were sitting in my father's living room after dinner when Jon's brain temporarily shut off and shriveled into a wrinkled mass the size of a green pea: he enthusiastically brought up a recent opinion piece about homosexuality he had read in the local newspaper. Once the word HOMO-SEXUALITY left Jon's mouth and exploded like a giant water balloon all over the room, both my father and I immediately shut down and receded to two different corners of the sofa.

There could not be a more uncomfortable conversation to have with my father, and in fact, I would almost rather talk about head lice. Neither he nor I said a word for the next twenty minutes because he knows he'll never change my mind, and me? I have seen his gun, and it is very gun-like.

Up until a few years ago I agreed with every perspective my father had on life. He raised me in a puritanical religion and taught me to believe very strict, very Republican principles. Nothing was more important than dignity and virtue and the feeling you get after an honest day's work, and those things are still very meaningful to me. But after college when I was out learning to make it on my own, I softened around the edges a bit. I stopped seeing things in such strict black-and-white lines. And then horror beyond horrors, *I started agreeing with Democrats.* I remember the touch-screen voting machine during the 2004 Presidential elections when I marked my choice for John Kerry, how I took a little too much pleasure knowing that when my father lay down to go to sleep that night, he'd linger a few seconds on the infuriating thought that because he had contributed to the birth of such a liberal daughter, he most likely has a sperm or two or twelve hundred in his body that, if given the chance, would vote in favor of gay marriage.

I imagine it's similar to the pleasure he experienced one evening around the dinner table years ago when I was three years old. He'd decided to use me, his youngest and most precious infant, in a scientific experiment, one that would determine what would happen when an innocent, helpless child reached for her apple juice only to guzzle several ounces of pickle juice. Just before we sat down to dinner, he replaced my cup of apple juice with the liquid of a Vlasic Dill Pickle jar, and then he waited for me to take a swig. He was so eager for me to knock back that pickle juice that he couldn't take a single bite of his own food. And then it happened, I inevitably became thirsty enough that I reached for a drink, and a single sip of that pickle juice caused a very angry host demon to shoot up through the top of my skull. My father thought it was the funniest thing he had ever seen, my pickle juice pain, and I remember thinking MY FATHER DOESN'T LOVE ME AND HAS JUST FED ME POISON. I wasn't the tiniest bit resentful for the next twenty-seven years. Not at all.

I swallow loudly and say, "Jon loves you, Dad." And then I ask without wanting to know the answer, "Why?"

"Does he really?" he asks. "How much does he love us?"

I guess not enough that he won't bring up The Gays in his living room, but that has nothing to do with love and everything to do with a terminal case of absentmindedness. Again, Jon is a saint when it comes to my family. He is the Official Troubleshooter for Anything Remotely Technical for all 100 Members of the Extended Armstrong and Hamilton Families Living in Utah, and routinely spends family gatherings helping someone find the shut-off valve to a sprinkler system or installing the driver for a new printer on a ten-year-old computer. My family can just go on with themselves about how gruesome and uncomely before the Lord I became when I abandoned my religious upbringing, but they know that if I were to walk away right now, I would take Jon with me, and nothing in their houses would ever be fixed again, particularly anything that requires downloading or an exe file or even a simple restart.

"He loves you like his own family," I say. And this is the

truth. Jon loves my father, particularly because Jon is the more conservative one in our relationship, and they see eye to eye more than is normal for a son and father-in-law. In fact, I think Jon considers my father an ally when it comes to coping with the curveballs I have a tendency to throw his way, particularly when it comes to the ways in which I take after my mother's side of the family, the side full of unnecessary drama and the unending need to discuss bodily functions.

My father does not abide the talk of things like excrement or snot and will get up and walk away from you if you so much as insinuate that humans poop. In fact, my father's sense of decorum cannot be overstated. Have I ever told you about that one time I heard my dad pass gas, and just as I was about to laugh, a red laser shot out of his eye and seared a 2-inch hole in my skull? I couldn't remember who I was for weeks. I still have a hard time remembering dates.

> *Have I ever told you about that one time I heard my dad pass gas, and just as I was about to laugh, a red laser shot out of his eye and seared a 2-inch hole in my skull?*

The first time Jon and my father realized they were on the same team, the one designated to deal with me, was the night that my father happened to be visiting on the same night that I had to give our two-year-old daughter a suppository for the first time.

Math had informed us before my father came over that the night would be a rough one because our daughter, Leta, had not properly gone to the bathroom in over seven days. I don't handle stress very well, especially poop stress, so instead of waiting and waiting for The Poop That Would Never Come, I opted to try out a suppository. I usually honor my father's preference to leave poop talk out of the conversation, but he was staying at my house and in my house HUMANS POOP.

After dinner and at precisely the most inconvenient time, that time being our Leta's bedtime and witching hour, I got up from the table and told Jon I'd be in her bedroom ENGAGING IN CERTAIN UNSAVORY ACTIVITIES, WINK WINK. Jon started to get up to come help me but I needed him to distract my father, to help my father forget that someone in the house was not only about to go poop but was going to be COAXED into going poop, a sin on par with being coaxed into felony misdemeanor.

I'd never inflicted a suppository on someone else, let alone a baby, that at the time no longer resembled a baby but more of a furry creature wreaking havoc on the ecosystem in the Australian Outback. I had to turn cartwheels to get that kid to sit still for 15 minutes while I injected a foreign object into her butt and held her cheeks shut. All I could think while I stood there, her little rubber butt in my hands, was oh my God, how many of my friends and relatives have done this very thing and then gone back to their normal lives as if they hadn't ever held someone else's butt closed? How can I go back to the life I once led, a life before the anally inserted suppository, without thinking, hey, I just held someone's butt closed for 15 minutes?

While I stood there closing her butt, nothing happened and nothing seemed like it was going to happen. THEN WHAT? You can't just insert a suppository, not have it work, AND THEN GO ON LIVING. I started to panic, and risking my father's permanent disdain, I ran out to the dining room with a waist-down-naked Leta, her bare butt closed in my palm.

"Jon. It's not working," I whined. "IT'S NOT WORKING. We're all going to die!"

Jon had seen the poop-panicked Heather on endless occasions and knew how to handle the situation, the first thing being to assure me, "Heather, we're not going to die. We're all going to live."

I ran back into Leta's bedroom, the irrational part of my brain talking, certain that Jon wasn't taking me seriously. Oh, we were going to die, all right. My baby was never going to poop again, and we'd all be dead.

Leta could sense my anxiety, and it was past her bedtime. Thus began the screaming. She wasn't screaming in pain, no. She was screaming because she was tired and wanted someone to rescue her from the crazed, butt-clenching lunatic. My father walked back to the bedroom to see if he could help in any way, to see why she was screaming so loudly, and I told him she was mostly tired and grumpy. He made an appropriate remark about how, shoot! They don't make suppositories for *that*!

Thanks, Dad. GO BACK TO YOUR POOPLESS WORLD WHILE I DIE.

Jon finally took charge of the situation, removed the demon from my arms, dressed her, and put her to bed WITH THE SUPPOSITORY STILL IN HER BUTT. I was having a hard time seeing straight at this point, and when I left her room to be with my father in the living room, he asked me, "Is everything okay?"

"We're putting her to bed and hoping that she wakes up

with poop in her diaper. If she wakes up and there isn't any poop in her diaper, Jon's going to take me to the emergency room tomorrow to have my brain removed."

The night passed without incident, and we only heard Leta's usual remodeling noises coming from her crib. I had visions of waking up to find Leta unconscious in a pool of poop: BABY NEARLY DROWNED BY SUPPOSITORY. But when we woke up, she was smiling, her diaper soiled normally, all of us still alive. My father toasted his orange juice to Jon that morning with, "You are a good man! Welcome to *this* family!"

Jon has never given my father a reason to question his loyalty to our family, his admirable devotion to an obviously crazy wife, which is why I'm shocked by my father's next question.

"Do you think he loves us enough that he would help us out if we needed it?" he asks.

My heart starts to break a little. "Of course! Whatever you need, Dad," I say, hoping that he understands that he is an important part of our lives. And is he ever. We cherish the fact that he has developed a relationship with Leta, that she has a chance to know her grandfather, something neither Jon nor I ever really had. And there was a time in my life when I was worried that this might not be possible, not because of distance or age, but because of differences that once threatened to tear me and my father apart.

Several years ago my father discovered things I had written on the Internet about my upbringing, bitter rants about religion and politics and the strict black-and-white teachings of my youth. I was very angry in my early twenties because I was still figuring things out, still trying to blame my insecurities on other people, and when he read those things, when he saw what I had become, he was destroyed. He phoned me one night, called me a few hurtful names, and then we didn't speak for three months.

It's not a time in my life that I like to think about, and not just because I'm ashamed of some of the ridiculous, alcohol-induced things I wrote. Now that I have a child of my own, I can feel the fullness of the pain that he went through watching his child reject so much of her upbringing. I even agree with some of the names he called me, because if my child ever did the same thing, I'D CALL HER SOMETHING WORSE. My father was right all along, and because I'm a parent now, because I am living the same sacrifices he made, I don't have to swallow any pride to admit that. My father now makes sense.

I want him to know that I love him as his child, but more importantly that as an adult I respect the man that he is.

"Jon would do anything for you," I finally answer.

"Good," he says. "Then tell him I have an angry skunk stuck in my window well, and I need someone to climb in and get him out."

I should have known, because not only did he teach me everything I know about finances and hard work and giving everything I've got, he taught me how to joke with clerks at the grocery store, how to find something to laugh about when confronted with something totally absurd, how to make someone else laugh at themselves. My sense of humor is his sense of humor. It is my father I see when I look in the mirror.

∾

*Heather B. Armstrong is the award-winning publisher of dooce®
(dooce.com). She gained notoriety in 2002 as one of the first people to
be fired because of a blog, and in 2005 dooce.com was chosen by* Time
magazine *as one of the 50 Coolest Websites. Armstrong has been on*
Good Morning America, *CNN, NPR, and* ABC's World
News Tonight *as a featured commenter on both blogging and post-
partum depression, as well as profiled in* The New York Times
Sunday Style *section and the* Washington Post Weekend Magazine.
She was published in Real Simple's *Family edition in August 2007.
Armstrong lives in Salt Lake City, Utah, with her husband, daughter,
and dog.*

What I Remember

Margaret Mason

I'm a writer, but I didn't write my father's eulogy; I'm not even sure he had an obituary. I was eight when he died.

I was staying over at Julie Tucker's house the night it happened, and my mother sent for me early. When I arrived home, my aunts were there, cleaning. I could smell bleach in the air.

"Did Grandpa die?" I asked.

My mother sat me down on my twin bed. It was freshly made, thanks to my aunts, covered in an unzipped Strawberry Shortcake sleeping bag.

"Dad is dead," my mother said.

Years later, I would think back on this moment when I heard of other people's tragedies. How these things happen, right in the middle of everything. How tragedy is both quotidian and unexpected.

For a long time, this baffled me—how people could keep going in the face of constant uncertainty. It was easy to imagine crucial changes unfolding in my most mundane moments.

"Are you asleep?" I asked Julie.

"No! Are you asleep?" she said.

At home, my father was dying on the couch.

ᗧ

When I had my son Henry twenty-three years later, I kept waiting to experience a new level of love. I waited to say things like, "I didn't even know what love *was* until my son was born." Or, "Everything changed from the moment I saw his tiny little hands."

But I never felt that way. I loved Hank just as much as I loved his father, and my sister, and my best friend. I loved him enough that it eclipsed me sometimes, but no more than that. I asked my husband Bryan about it.

"You know how everyone says that you don't really know what love is until you have a baby?"

"Yeah."

"How you'll love your baby more than you've ever loved anything else?"

"Yeah."

"Do you feel that way? Like you love Hank more than you've ever loved anything, ever, in your whole life?"

"Not really."

"Me neither. I have a theory about it."

"Okay."

"You know how when you have a baby, you worry a lot about things that could kill the baby?"

"Mmmhmm."

"I think people who've never lost someone close to them

don't know what that's like. They have a baby, and it's the first time they realize that someone so important to them could die. They have no idea what might happen."

By the time Henry came along, I was excellent at the What Might Happen game. I had been playing it with his father's life for five years.

What will I do if Bryan stops breathing right now? I would think while we were lying together in bed. *What will I say if he calls from the plane to say it's going down? How will I find him if there's an earthquake?*

Five photos of my father:

1. He is a kid, about nine years old, and his hair is so blond it's nearly white. His hands are in fists on his hips, and he's twisted awkwardly toward the camera with his eyes crossed and his cheeks puffed out.
2. He is next to a tank in Vietnam wearing drab green pants and a white undershirt. You can just make out his dog tags.
3. He is inside a large metal tube, pretending to be sucked into it. He's wearing coveralls. The tube must be some sort of airplane part—maybe the cylinder that holds the propellers under the wings? His eyes are rolled back into his head, and his mouth is open in a dramatic yowl.
4. Dad's hair is brown and curly now, a messy puff that stands out from his head in every direction. His face is calm, thoughtful. I'm about two, and he's holding me on

his lap next to a public fountain. I've been splashing in the water and am naked.

5. He is sitting with me and Mom on the living room couch. We're in holiday clothes and Dad is leaning back with his arm around Mom. His free hand is throwing a mock gang sign at the camera.

A few facts about my father:

He died when he was thirty-four. He was overweight, and he smoked, and he hid Hershey bars in the glove compartment of our old Volkswagen van. They melted in the summer heat, and when I was playing in the car, I would lick them out of their wrappers.

His eyes were blue, and he had a moustache. I never dated a man with facial hair, because the idea of feeling that paternal prickle when I kissed them always made me cringe.

He teased people. He waited until my especially polite girlfriends had taken a bite of food before asking them questions. They would chew, swallow, and then answer. He'd pause, wait for them to take another bite, then ask another question.

When he was little, his older brother was hard on him. Cruel to him, my mother said. Once, a neighborhood bully pushed my younger cousin and me into the gutter and wouldn't let us back up. We returned home crying, and my dad asked what was wrong. His face turned purple when we told him. He left immediately for the boy's house. Whatever was said, the kid never touched me again. Never even made eye contact.

Dad played Andrews Sisters records, but Bing Crosby was his favorite. His wedding ring was a simple gold band. He slept on the couch; Mom said it was because he snored. On Saturday nights, I would lie next to him on the couch and he let me stay up so we could watch *Saturday Night Live*. He loved John Belushi. I mostly fell asleep on top of him, with my cheek pressed against his white T-shirt. Sometimes he fell asleep watching TV, too, and I woke to study his face in the flicker of the TV screen.

He was an excellent whistler, the kind who can whistle through his teeth. He drummed on the steering wheel while he drove, and played a *Jim Croce's Greatest Hits* tape over and over. If it was dark when we pulled in the driveway, I would pretend to be asleep so he would carry me inside.

His fingernails were short. He worked nights as a jet engine mechanic for the Air Force. He fixed all our cars, and convinced my mom to let him buy a Mercedes shortly before he died. It was a 1975, gold 450SEL. About seven years later it became my first car, though by that time it was blue and the springs were poking up through decaying leather seats.

He was solid, a hard worker. Until the Friday before he died, he had never called in sick to work.

Dad was the disciplinarian in our family. The one who spanked, devised equitable punishments, looked at me sternly when I deserved it. If I left orange peels or apple cores lying around (as I often did), he made me carry them everywhere for half an hour, so I would remember to put them in the garbage the next time.

When my parents' friends started the first wave of divorces in my youth, I remember thinking that I'd rather go with my mom if my parents got divorced, because Dad was meaner.

After he died, that impulsive thought made my brain itch, I couldn't seem to forgive myself.

❧

One of my earliest memories is my parents' faces looming over me, trying to figure out whether I'm telling the truth.

Dad says, "I think she's lying."

Mom says, "I don't think she knows *how* to lie."

I am lying.

I remember Dad tickling me until I could barely breathe. He smelled like clean laundry.

> *I remember Dad tickling me until I could barely breathe. He smelled like clean laundry.*

I remember sitting on his lap looking down at my legs. I am wearing a white Swiss dot dress with a red ribbon sash, patent leather shoes. His arm is wrapped around my tummy.

When I was four, we took a Universal Studios Tour. The *Jaws* robot leaped from the water as the tram tipped sideways a bit, and I shrieked. The whole bus turned to look. As my eyes began to brim, Dad put his hand to his throat.

"Ahem," he said. "Excuse me."

❧

Margaret Mason is author of No One Cares What You Had for Lunch: 100 Ideas for Your Blog *(Peachpit). Her shopping blog, Mighty Goods (www.mightygoods.com), was one of* Time Magazine's Top 50 Cool Sites of the Year, *and was named Best Shopping Site by* Forbes *and* BusinessWeek. *Since 2000, her personal site Mighty Girl (www.mightygirl.com) has drawn thousands of readers each day.*

Hostage

Jon Armstrong

Right out of university one of the partners at my job mentioned casually that he was trying to figure out if I was the way I was because of my father or in spite of my father. Since my father was dead, I safely replied, "Both."

Another partner at that same firm told me a few weeks later that I was a cultural anomaly.

At the time of my supposed cultural peculiarity, I was unshackled by the mandatory grooming code at my alma mater, Brigham Young University, and had begun a series of hair experimentations involving the face and scalp that would have likely driven my father bananas. I was also in a band at the time, which was perfect cover for looking simultaneously like a hipster and a homeless person dressed in borrowed clothes to hold down a day job.

As part of the experimentation, I wore clothing bearing a misspelling of the past perfect superlative of the acronym "for unlawful carnal knowledge" and T-shirts with dead extremists on them. This would not be greeted with wondrous glee were my father alive and able to comment about how I was going to hell and/or getting a swift kick in the ass.

When I was a kid, I heard my father express countless times just how hard he was going to kick any of my brothers' asses and where they'd be wearing the ass once he was done. Generally in the ear area of the head. I wasn't supposed to find this humorous in the moment, but I couldn't help thinking that my brothers would look really funny wearing their asses up high like that. Especially as I watched from the sidelines with full immunity. As I got older and the immunity faded, I had severe dread about the look and the temper. It's funny now, but in the moment, the overriding emotion wasn't "ha-ha," it was "keep your shit together or you'll be next."

Born in the mid-1920s, my father was part of what is now referred to as the "Greatest Generation." He married my mother when he was twenty-one and she was seventeen. He was in the United States Navy Reserve at the end of World War II and was called up at the end of the Korean War. Part of his generational zeitgeist meant men had to know certain things and perform certain tasks lest a man be considered something less. He fathered six children with my mother, three boys and three girls. My younger sister Kathryn and I were surprise children. The age gap between my next oldest brother, Tom, and Kathryn is ten years. Between me and my oldest brother, Kesler, the age gap is fourteen years.

When we mostly nonhooligan but hyper boys didn't perform to muster, there was hell to pay and my father's generation didn't stand for things like "feelings," "approval," "validation," "feeling vulnerable," or "being threatened," or "requiring gobs of therapy after a failed first marriage." When my dad said

move, you moved. Immediately. In my adolescence, my friends
were considered slightly above heroin addicts and referred to
as dumb-asses until they earned a better designation. Compared
to the seventeen-year-olds he knew and sailed across the Pacific
with, we *were* dumb-asses. My dad was a hard ass, plain and
simple. It wasn't so much that he was battle tested or scarred as
much as it was generational. It was expected that when your
kids misbehaved, you spanked them. Physical threats and fol-
low-through were normal. My brothers and I were in that line
of fire every day. A big part of me wants to absolve my father
by saying that he wasn't physically abusive. But he was. I
watched him kick and hit my older brothers far more than he
did with me. I was hit exactly once. Spanked too numerous to
count, but hit only once after I protested brat-like behavior
from my younger sister and pushed her a little too hard. She
could play in the NBA with the histrionics she pulled that day,
which made the hit seem even more needless. Of course, I ex-
acted revenge on my younger sister. And steered clear of my
dad's fists.

Despite the environment of fear, I never did nor have done
anything to spite my father. I didn't resent him or what he
stood for. It was never like that. I don't think he was fully comfortable with the way the country moved in the 1960s and
early '70s. He could see that I was a product of the shift in
thinking about the environment, personal expression, and loud
music. Watergate and the Vietnam War didn't help, either. I
couldn't fully understand this shift, but I remember the dinner
conversations with my older siblings and anybody who questioned. I wasn't angry he died when he did as much as I was
sad that he'd never meet people in my future. He'd never see

wives, children, friends, or dogs. He'd never tell me that I paid too much for that car or house. He'd never come over to my house for dinner and talk about politics and how you are supposed to vote the party line. I'd miss getting yelled at for voting for Clinton twice. He'd miss seeing my young family and the granddaughter that looks so much like him.

As a creative type, I clashed more than got along with him, and it was really awkward for me to discover toward the end of his life that my dad was actually a creative soul as well, he just took a different, more easily respected path in life. He and I likely had more than our looks in common. He'd probably hate that I'm writing this, but secretly like the fact that I have.

Saturday afternoons, when other kids were out playing, I'd be forced as a kind of hostage to work with my dad on projects that he endlessly puttered before getting to. He'd start the day gathering bits and pieces. I'd notice his scavenging out of the corner of my eye while watching my power block of Saturday morning cartoons that started at 7 A.M. and went on for four hours. We had one TV in the house then. With eight people in the house, it was impossible to schedule time, so I'd wake up early. I had developed a finely tuned anger radar, and if I saw a bogey approaching, I could scramble. I'd mash the "off" button on the TV and run to my room, pretending to be very busy dressing myself or maybe making my bed if I really wanted to score some points.

My father had a short fuse. Living with explosives, one learns to sense the danger and develop contingency plans. Not that any of my scheming actually worked.

My father had a short fuse. Living with explosives, one learns to sense the danger and develop contingency plans. Not that any of my scheming actually worked.

I'd usually be forced on a trip to the hardware store for project materials and a tangential conversation with the owner or other putterers. My dad was on the city council, and if he saw stakeholders or players, he'd stop and talk. My father was a long talker. He didn't talk big. He was too diplomatic for that. He talked long. He'd corral people and think nothing of a thirty-minute conversation, to hell with the bored children in tow.

After surviving the hardware store, it was home for a beverage (nonalcoholic) and perhaps a diversion to the news or sporting event being broadcast live. Then lunch. I'd need to be on call and close by. Usually I'd have fielded a couple of calls from friends and tried to skive off working with my dad, but it never worked. I was trapped.

We'd finally get going on the project at about 2:30 and we'd work until 6 or so. During these project days, I'd get stories from my dad about the past, history lessons, the odd swear word from a missed nail, or battles with flimsy plaster walls that hadn't been covered in canvas and skimmed, so they flaked when nailed, drilled, or were looked at wrongly. And they deserved the cussing out. More often than not, I'd be the gofer and have to locate extension cords, lost screwdrivers, drill bits, and misplaced sockets. I dreaded not knowing where something was. If my dad had to stop work and go find it himself, I'd be subject to a barrage of insults, harangues, and curses. My father never used the worst words, and his inventions and contortions of language were meant to scare me and stop him from fully sinning. God was not an allowed swear word.

"Gad dammit!"

"Bugger Damn!"

"Hellfreeze!"

Maybe his rage wasn't from the work itself, but trying to avoid using the words he really wanted to. I never heard him say the f-word. It always surprised me that I learned how to drop f-bombs from my friends and not my dad. He was in the military. He knew the bad words. But he was also Mormon, something he came to after he had married my mom. Bad words weren't just bad, they kept you from God.

My dad sensed in me that I didn't want to be working with him. He had to see it. It would be cold outside in November when he'd enlist me for the annual draining of the radiator in the station wagon or in the brittle January working in the un-heated basement of our hundred-year-old house. At twelve, I didn't know enough trigonometry to measure and calculate the perfect starting 45° angle position for the parquet floor we were to install in the entryway. I wasn't good with tools, at least that's the impression I got. I worked too slowly. I didn't hold the hammer the right way. I hated screwing up and making him angry. It wasn't fun or funny. I know a couple of therapists who are better off because of the impact of these Saturdays with him. He'd sense me drifting off to an imaginary playtime and that is when I'd get treated, for the thousandth time, to the stories from when he was younger. The Depression and finish-ing every last item on his plate or getting smacked with a knife across his knuckles for reaching across the table. He scraped through college on the GI Bill, having to work part-time jobs to pay the other bills. "We were poor, Jon."

He didn't say this sadly. It was more subtle than that. He would talk about how working Saturdays during his college years at a gas station/repair shop meant he couldn't attend football games and how he'd hear the roar of the crowd from his job and want to be at the game. He talked about this with a kind of pride and a regret I have never forgotten. Knowing he was poor and had to work hard to give me a comparative life of luxury didn't make those Saturdays any easier.

Lest you think that I was raised in shackles and routinely beaten before being shoved in my cage for a meal of gruel followed by a night of tears and lack of sleep due to a burgeoning relationship with an imaginary and/or fictional rodent cellmate, you should know my father attended every play, every band performance, and supported my early publishing efforts. Including a time when I used two of the four Latin words I knew (vas deferens) to describe something in an editorial piece. He cried silently when we got our new piano during an impromptu recital by me and Kathryn. I believe he also cried in 1980 when the U.S. hockey team beat the Russian hockey team. He'd tear up other times, but it was pretty rare to see that kind of emotion displayed, and when it was, it was always quiet and barely detectable. The only time I ever saw him really cry in public was the first Mother's Day at church after his own mother died. He was speaking in front of the congregation and lost it. He hadn't grieved much about her dying and I had expected him to open up at some point. It took four months.

Around this time, my father's illness began to manifest, but no one except my mom caught it. She was terrified that it was Alzheimer's and was paralyzed thinking that my father was losing it. She didn't talk about this to anyone for a year. He just seemed a little off, a little more distant. He had just lost his mother, so could you blame him? But my mom knew. As a person in my late teens at the time, I was too self-absorbed to notice anything other than my desire to move on with my life.

When it came time to choose my path after high school, it was a given that I'd attend a university. My parents were terrified that I wouldn't serve a Mormon mission and at every turn were recommending a school close enough for me to commute to and live at home. They wanted to monitor me so the devil wouldn't talk me out of a righteous life. My brother Tom had dropped out after two terms and they didn't want a repeat. They blamed it on partying, which may have been partly true, but Tom wasn't into the university scene.

I chose to attend Utah State University and moved away to "learn the basic tasks one needs to cope in life, you know, in case I decide to go on a mission." They begrudgingly bought it. Or pretended to buy it. I chose a difficult major to prove that I was serious. So serious that for two terms, I bombed the hell out of my freshman year.

After the implosion—nearly getting thrown out of school and only being readmitted under counsellor supervision—I had a good quarter and then decided to go on the Mormon mission my parents so wanted. I had decided that one of the reasons I did so poorly in school was that the university I had chosen wasn't a good fit for me because I wanted to get far away from my small town. Mormon missionaries from Utah often get sent far away when they get their assignment. The mission option was a gamble, but I got lucky and was sent to Manchester, England. I don't know if my father was ever more proud of me. Even though I've since left the faith, I still view going to England as a gift to myself and a gift to him. That he paid for out of his own pocket.

Mormon missions are served at the expense of the missionary. All of the ministry in Mormondom is a lay ministry. People are called from the congregation to serve. There is no collection plate per se. If called for any position, one is expected to accept and serve. Missions are voluntary, so it is expected that if a person chooses to serve a mission, the missionary or the family of the missionary will bear the cost. At the time that I left in late 1984, the average 18-month mission to England was expected to cost $3,600 US. Double that if you were assigned a car and had to pay for your own petrol. That was with the fantastic exchange rate of the mid-eighties that lasted for the first month I was out, but got steadily worse as my mission time passed. I'd put the total cost for my mission around $7,000 US. My dad gladly paid my way. I tried to do him proud. I think I succeeded for the most part, despite my unorthodox method of using popular culture, particularly music, to start conversations with people in an attempt to try to show a less dour and fervent side of the religion.

Right around the midpoint of my mission time, around the nine-month mark, my dad's illness could no longer be ignored. He was diagnosed with a brain tumor and rushed into emergency surgery. I found out about the surgery as it was happening from the leader of the mission, the mission president. I got a call late one July evening and was told to come into the president's office first thing the next day. This was in the days when there was no e-mail or cell phone service for normal people. As a missionary, I wasn't allowed to call home unless I had permission. That morning, the president gave me the news and told me that my father had gone into surgery. I'd be allowed to call home at 3 P.M. England time. He told me to go out and work and come back to make the call. He'd give me his office in private to speak to my family.

I had no idea if my father would survive the surgery. I had no idea if I'd be able to stay in England if my dad didn't pull through. I spent the next six hours in agony. At the time, I was training a new missionary and I was useless that day. I'd try to keep in good spirits, but I purposefully took longer-than-normal bus rides to our work areas so that I wouldn't have to deal with people. Mormons are very big on doing the Lord's work to get over things. It didn't take with me.

I made it back into the president's office and all the staff handled me in a way that did not bode well. I was terrified that my father had died. I decided to put that thought out of my head and be ready for anything as I dialed home.

My father survived the surgery. Huge relief. However, given the nature of brain tumors, the doctors weren't sure until he recovered how much higher brain function he would have. The tumor was sizable. I didn't even hear the size of the tumor, whether or not it was related to his prostate cancer from ten years prior, or much of anything else. He was alive. My mother told me, as did all of my siblings that day, that my father had expressed on his way into surgery that he wanted me to stay in England and finish the mission. My family supported his wishes, and despite being torn, I decided to wait it out and see what happened.

I served the remaining 9 of the 18 months I had signed up for and my dad recovered from surgery, eventually returning to work for a short time. I decided that I didn't need permission to take calls from my family and made sure that whatever flat I was in, they knew my number and city code. I spoke to my father a few times in those months and was buoyed by his spirit and almost normal ability to speak and carry on conversation. Despite the signs that he was recovering, it was very difficult to live each day to its fullest knowing that at any moment I might get a call that he was worsening.

In April 1986 I finished my mission and returned to Utah. I had a rude awakening with my dad's state and life at home. He wasn't who he was when I left. Those great phone calls couldn't show me how he walked with a cane sometimes or the scars from the surgery. He had a slight list when he walked and was on somebody's arm most of the time.

My dad still had his anger and rages; the fuse was still just as short. But the surgery had done something to him. After he'd yell, my mother would tell him he didn't need to be so loud (she never did this before he got sick), and he'd respond by whispering his next few sentences.

During this time, I had an opportunity to move out and get restarted with my life. That April I spent a few weeks in turmoil trying to decide whether I should stay and help my mom or get going with my life. At the time, I had thought that my dad would survive for years like this: sick, but not terminal. Maybe he wasn't able to work anymore, but certainly he was not dying anytime soon. Even in England, I hadn't faced such a difficult decision. He was mostly lucid, but needed constant care. My father's wishes were that he not be hospitalized. He wanted to die at home. My mom told me with tears in her eyes she'd understand if I left, but if I did, I'd miss the beauty of seeing my father die. She'd never been that poetic before. And I'd never looked at it like that before. Death was not beautiful. I stayed home to help my mother and I spent the next four months finding the beauty in my father's death.

Toward the end, he became more childlike, and while it was sad, it was also glorious. He disappeared one day. He wandered a couple of blocks to downtown to get his funeral portrait taken without telling anybody. When the photographer called up a few hours later to mention that maybe somebody needed to come get my dad, we were relieved, but it meant we'd have to be more vigilant. I often wonder how much conversation the photographer took before making that call.

After a few weeks, it was clear that he was deteriorating. I had to clean and shave him in his bed on those days when he had visitors. He had lost the ability to bathe himself. We had developed a strange bond in those last months. I got up the nerve to tell him that I loved him. I had never said that to his face. He told me he loved me back, something he had rarely told me and, given our clashes in the past, something I needed to hear before he died.

To get through these rough days, we had taken to gathering in my father's room at night as a family to wish him good-night. Oftentimes various siblings would be there, making the room crowded. The room was unnaturally dark with 1970s paneling and a couple of dim antique lamps that cast long shadows up the walls and onto the ceiling. Being in that room was like going back in time. In the lamplight, it wasn't hard to feel the history of these last days with my father. One night in July, right before I turned twenty-one, I was kneeling at his bedside to pray. During the prayer, he put his hand on my head as if I were a toddler and rubbed it gently until the prayer was over. I never wanted that prayer to end. I felt I never had enough of that kind of love from him as a kid and I was going to miss it as an adult. He died a few weeks later, spending those last weeks in silence as he had lost the ability to speak. He didn't give me any parting wisdom or final words. However, his death, like a human lathe, spun and shaped every major decision that followed in my adult life.

Jon Armstrong is a consultant, designer, art director, photographer, nerd dilettante, and sometime writer living in Salt Lake City, Utah, with his wife, daughter, and dog. He is a Democrat. His father was a staunch Republican and likely rolling in his grave at the mention that his youngest son refuses to carry on the tradition. Armstrong has a blog, blurbomat, at http://www.blurbomat.com, and is a sometime contributor to the music site 3hive at http://www.3hive.com. He has been published in grid *magazine,* URB, Red Herring, *and* JPG.

Finding My Father

Leah Peterson

All my experiences with my father up until my late twenties are colored with a very specific lens. He was a good man. A quiet man. A complicated man. I don't mean to talk about my dad in the past tense. He is very much alive. But something about the nature of his disease makes me look at the reality of him now and see him using my filters of five years ago, ten years ago. Dementia can do that.

When I was growing up, my brain was not quite right. Disordered. My family made many allowances to keep me included in their midst. It was difficult because every action I made screamed rebellion and most words out of my mouth went well beyond the basic teenager routine. My father's brain was sharp as a tack. He was a word-twister: quick with spoonerisms; twisting the beginnings of words and saying "flutterby" for "butterfly" and "Nun-day Might!" for "Monday Night." He memorized hundreds of poems, which he recited at many family gatherings. His sense of humor was corny but we genuinely laughed when he threw toothpicks in the water glasses and called them Pine Floats.

Today, my mind is no longer disordered. My father, however, recites poems with my mother standing by, prompting
him. We don't love him any less. Just like my family loved me
in spite of my drama and acting out. Our brains are not the entire story or assessment of our worth as humans.

> *Our brains are not the entire story or assessment of our
> worth as humans.*

I spent many years trying to find my father, even when he
lived in the same home as me. He was elusive. Sometimes I
could see him but I couldn't feel him. Sometimes I didn't see
him at all when my mind played tricks on me. Being a doctor,
he used what he knew to perform surgical procedures on me
that instead of helping me to stop wetting the bed, in fact hurt
me quite a bit and caused my brain to split and dissociate from
the pain of the situation. I would spend the next twenty-five
years recovering from those procedures and other situations
that stemmed from them. I had low self-esteem and poor
boundaries as a child and teenager. I wore an invisible WEL-
COME sign that would-be perpetrators would see like a flashing
neon sign and I never quite knew when people were stepping
on my rights as a human being. I lived through different mo-
lestations and date-rape situations until I finally married. I still
struggle today with some issues. But not in finding my love for
him, my father. No, I reclaimed my love for him at the same
time that I was able to forgive him.

One summer, when I was around eight years old, my father
drove the family to Canada. We loaded up the Suburban,
which was the only vehicle we all fit in at the time, and started
driving. It crossed my mind that we had never driven this far

away from home and I wondered if my dad really knew which way to go. "All the way to Canada" seemed as far as the other end of the earth. And the prospect of sitting wedged between two older siblings for three entire days did not seem all that appealing.

Within a few miles of driving on old Highway 89, I threw up. Being carsick was kind of a staple activity of mine but I endeavored to keep any from splashing on anyone's clothing or the seats. I should mention that because I always failed at these two things, I sometimes had more room surrounding me than anyone else in the car.

My father would give me Dramamine, hoping to keep my tumbling stomach at bay. Great intention on his part. It would have been very helpful, too, if I could have taken pills without triggering the gag reflex. But things being how they were, I was afraid to take the pills for fear I would gag and throw up, and then I threw up because I didn't take the pills. I was in a quandary for my father. I was feeling rather old at age eight, and for this particular drive, instead of telling him I wouldn't take the Dramamine, I palmed the tiny pill, stuffed it in my pocket, and flushed it in a gas station bathroom stall.

After driving down the winding, twisting road for just over an hour, my upset stomach got the best of me, and suddenly, the inside of the Suburban smelled like sour vomit. My father stopped at a drugstore and my mother ran in and purchased a lemon-scented pop-up air freshener. She peeled the covering off the adhesive on the back, popped open the top, and stuck that sucker on the wall of the car right next to where I was sitting. I could see my father's eyes in the rearview mirror and I felt very sorry to have caused such a problem and even sorrier that I had to sit next to the overpowering scent of lemon for the three days it took to drive to Ontario.

A week later when we drove home, the lemon scent had faded, but just barely. I was able to enjoy Old Faithful, which incidentally was not faithfully on time, as my father pointed out, and hadn't been for years, without thinking of clean kitchens and lemon trees. The same cannot be said for our stop at Mount Rushmore the day after The Vomit, where I swear the eyes on President Jefferson were quite lemon-shaped.

Time has a way of healing all wounds and fading lemon-scented air fresheners. The smell of my vomit never did actually leave that Suburban, wiped seats and lemon scent notwithstanding. It was my way of christening a vehicle, since I upchucked in every one we ever owned at least twice, including the station wagon with the fake wood paneling that someone named Lurch due to a faulty and testy transmission. Lurch stopped working every trip we ever took to Arizona, right after we left the populated areas and entered a stretch of desolate road. My father spent a lot of time walking in one direction or another looking for help. I didn't always hate it when we broke down, though, because sometimes, if we were lucky, we'd come to a stop near one of the Indian jewelry stands and my dad would buy me a turquoise ring or bracelet. Despite the troubles between us, I loved when he did something like that.

Throughout our Canada adventure, besides the vomiting, and besides the afternoon somewhere near the border when my mom made us all peanut butter and jelly sandwiches on her knees according to our specific orders and my sister called out "peanut butter and jelly—hold the bread!," the things that stand out strongest are about my father. The anomalies.

Mostly, because being stuck in a car for days will show you sides of people you never knew existed.

My dad had a deep baritone voice but could also sing tenor. My family has been known to sing a song or two while driving late at night, mostly I think to help keep my father awake, but when I was young, staring out the window, my head on a small-sized travel pillow with a tan corduroy cover slowly pressing creases into my cheek, gazing at millions of bright stars overhead and listening to my mom and dad harmonize, with my siblings joining in with the alto and soprano, I had no inkling we were engaging in a safety feature that would ensure our safe passage. I just thought it was the most beautiful thing I'd ever heard when my dad started singing "*Oh Danny Boy.*"

On another night of that same trip, we were somewhere in the Midwestern states, when my dad started chuckling and announced that the bumper sticker on the car in front of him said, DIM DEM DAMN LIGHTS! Cars driving behind him with their brights on were a pet peeve of my father's and we heard him remark a few times an hour about one car or another. Seeing this bumper sticker really cracked him up. It's unfortunate that he had raised all us kids in such a sheltered environment, which included curse words being very high on the list of Do Nots, because we did not laugh. Not only did we not laugh, my sister told him how horrible it was that he had read such a thing out loud and then laughed about it. My mom asked him to apologize to everyone in the car. I started crying not only for the soul of my father but for all the people that lived in these heathen central states who had created such an abomination. It put quite a damper on the evening. I'd just like to mention that I still remember said bumper sticker thirty years later, so you have to hand it to whoever created it with such marketing longevity, even though my memory might be entirely situational. It also occurs to me that much of this trip was spent with my father apologizing.

I've heard my father curse only one other time my entire life and it was the summer after Canada. He had been mowing the lawn with our electric lawn mower and ran over the cord with the blades. The protective rubber covering had been shaved off over a stretch of a few inches. My father picked up the cord and accidentally got too close to the exposed wires, and suddenly, he had a large number of volts coursing through his veins. His teeth chattering, he tried to yell, "Unplug the cord, dammit!" But it really didn't come out all that loud, although it was at least loud enough for me to hear him swear and for my brother to pull the cord from the socket.

My father was not a swearing kind of individual, which is why these incidents stand out so clearly. At my young age, I wanted to think he was perfect. I already had proof in the physical form of my aching tiny lady parts after every medical procedure to improve my bladder that my father was capable of hurting me. But I somehow thought of them as isolated events, separate from the rest of his life. When these swearing incidents happened, I noticed them so much simply because they were little digs into my brain. Reminders that my father was not, in fact, a perfect man. I would spend years rolling these imperfections of him around in my mind, testing them to see how strong they were up against what I wanted to believe he was.

When I was eight, my father seemed very tall. I suppose it's not surprising for a human of four and a half feet in height to feel dwarfed by someone over six feet. But I don't think that is the only reason he seemed so tall to me. He was a man of conviction and he became passionate about things like our Church and our Country. It was fascinating to watch him once he took hold of a subject close to his heart because his face would light up and his eyes would get fierce. He just wanted others to see the same things he could see. And sometimes he would cry and there was something so wonderful about seeing those tears slide down his cheeks. It felt like a connection to him. Something real. When he was like that, he seemed to be about ten feet tall and I was in awe.

My father was a busy man. Not in the man-about-town way. He wasn't attending cocktail parties and going to the movies. He had a small circle of close friends and most of them didn't even live in town. But he seemed to be everywhere at once, volunteering in the community and helping people out. Even now he is a vibrant member of his town and spends hours cleaning up the sides of the roads in and out of the city lines. He has his own key to the city dump. That is how much he cleans.

When he wasn't cleaning up trash and weeds, he was using his spare time to garden or hike. He took good care of his neighbors and volunteered for church callings. And he spent long hours on call at the hospital and the clinic as he was one of only two or three doctors in town. Looking back, I think he kept himself busy because being idle made him feel uneasy, like he was wasting his precious life if he spent too much of it in one spot. He could barely sit still long enough to watch an entire broadcast of the news. Sometimes, as I'm trying to watch a movie on HBO while knitting, reading e-mail, texting the kids, and writing two short stories simultaneously in my head, I feel very close to him.

To say I was a little different as a child than I am now would be a gross misrepresentation of the highest magnitude. As an adult, I've had quite a few traits of my father's manifest in my personality, including his silly sense of humor, his to-the-point communication, his temper, his restlessness, and his work ethic. When I was young, mostly I was incommunicative and hiding from my chores and spending hours avoiding contact with him at any cost.

In the summers, my father gave us jobs to do in the garden or the yard. We lived on about an acre of land, which included fruit trees, raised garden beds, the occasional farm animal, large lawns, and a long portion of carport cement. All of this required maintenance and we were expected to do our part. Of all the children, I think it's safe to say that I was the most challenging in this area. If my chore was sweeping the carport, it would take me the better part of a week, most of which was spent talking to the broom handle explaining why I shouldn't be forced to work. Mowing the lawns would take at least an entire day, during which I sat on the grass a lot, looking at the mower and willing it to move itself. I remember reading *The Littles* books one summer and actively looking under clover and rocks trying to find the little people. I wanted to ask them to gather their tiny friends and do my work for me in exchange for a regular supply of cold cereal we had in the food storage room.

The summer when I was close to twelve, my dad asked me to paint the fence that went around the perimeter of our property as my summer job. I believe he was paying me an obscene wage per hour for those days, somewhere in the vicinity of seven or eight dollars. This was supposed to be an incentive to help keep me interested in my work. And normally, it would have worked. Other kids would have looked at the potential money and devised a plan on how to earn the maximum amount of money possible by painting a certain number of boards per day. Not too many and not too few. Sadly, that summer was the same summer I discovered Phyllis A. Whitney novels. Sitting in the barn reading seemed so much better than opening 10-gallon drums of khaki-colored paint and standing in the Southern Utah heat for hours a day painting a stupid fence. All told, I earned about forty dollars and painted close to 14 of the over 320 boards by August. My dad finished painting the fence during the last week of summer. He did it alone and in two days.

It's unfortunate for both of us that he happened to be so instrumental in the development of my brain disorder. There he was, a father trying to take care of his ailing child, and actually making things much worse. He and I missed out on many years as friends as a result of that. He could be very thoughtful, and after I had married and moved away, he sent me flowers when he knew I was having a hard time. And my scrapbook has a Valentine from him for every year starting from when I was about five, all signed "Love, Dad." He was and is a very fine dancer and on more than one occasion I went with him to events as a stand-in for my mother. During those times, I longed to feel close to him, but didn't, and resented him because talking with him and being with him were hard and took energy, and I didn't understand why. The very nature of my mind splitting meant that many of the reasons *why* I was angry at him had vanished into the recesses of my brain. There was no *why* to be found. I was just hurt and angry and acted out without understanding the reasons behind it.

I remember years of avoiding him. I hid when he came home from work and dreaded the time in the evening when I was expected to give him a kiss on the cheek and a hug before bed. He really wanted a way to connect with me and sometimes the nightly hug-and-kiss routine was the only moment he saw me in 24 hours. Years later while visiting home and after finding my love for him, I assumed his role. I would go to him and say in his own words, "Hey! I don't think I've had my hug today!"—and then plant a kiss on his cheek and give him a squeeze. He wouldn't always ask anymore. Dementia had made him unsure and he hated to repeat something so he just kind of looked at me with a question in his eyes and I wasted no time in closing the gap to give him a hug.

I notice with my own children, three of whom are boys, that wrangling a kiss and a hug can sometimes take bribery, manipulation, and weeping, all by me, and it's a miracle if I can get all of them to do it in one day. My children and I have our own hard history to overcome and I assume, conservatively, that they might be in their thirties before initiating the hugs entirely of their own volition. But that's all right. I can wait. I've learned patience from my father.

Of all the days I remember my dad for, the one when I called to tell him I was pregnant at seventeen years old seems to rise to the top. I had found out earlier in the day that I was for sure expecting and my body contained a fetus of about nine or ten weeks. I was confused, angry, in shock, and generally not much myself. I agonized about calling him because just two weeks prior he had sent me about a thousand dollars to register for classes at a community college with high school courses. I had planned to accelerate my learning and finish my junior and senior years at the same time by summer. For some reason, the fact that I was pregnant automatically meant I would be dropping out of school to get married and become a wife. At least I'm guessing that is what I thought, since I really have no good reason for connecting those two dots, and frankly, I don't remember really thinking it through. I suppose it was my religious upbringing that when a woman started having children, she stayed home and became a homemaker. In any case, what I told my father over the phone was something like, "Dad, I'm calling to tell you I'm so sorry about the money you just gave me for school because I'm dropping out." And just as he started to say, "You're WHA—?" I interrupted with, "I'm pregnant."

I was expecting the worst, probably some anger and yelling from him. He'd had it with my attitude and rebellion by that point, and I assumed that he would be so angry he would possibly hang up on me. With the exception of when I was very small, I was never so vulnerable and open to his feelings about me as I was in that moment. If he hated me, I wouldn't blame him. I hated myself.

Instead, my father said quietly, "Well, Leah, we all make mistakes. This is a big one, but I love you and we'll figure it out." After which I wept for a very long time and marveled that those words had come out of the same man that I knew as my father. It was the first time I ever thought that maybe all the horrible things I thought about him might not be completely accurate. Maybe he did love me. Maybe some of what we had gone through hadn't been entirely his fault. Maybe it was time to start taking some responsibility over my own life and quit reacting and acting out. I had a long, long way to go before I would be through the major parts of recovering from my childhood. But realizing these things was a very important first step.

I've had a number of people say they're astounded that my father and I are now friends. That I love him. That I forgave him. I suppose a lot of that comes with just growing up and realizing that your parents are real people. Just regular people with their own problems and that they wake up every day, the same as you, and hope they do the right things for their children. They make mistakes. I make mistakes. And we try to fix them as best we can as we go along.

Had my case with my father been an overtly sexual abuse case, I'm sure this part of our story would be different. There were people who sexually abused me when I was a child and I can tell you plain and simple—I do not want to be friends with them and I do not forgive them. However, I am no longer angry with them and I don't hold resentment or hate in my heart because I've learned that, for me, it just hurts me and makes my life hell. I've let it all go as best I can.

With my father, he thought the treatments he gave me for wetting the bed were helping me. He thought he was doing the best thing for me. He was wrong, but he wasn't evil. People ask me how I can be so sure. How can I know for certain that he wasn't doing it on purpose or that he's sorry about what happened?

My dad's parents both had dementia toward the end of their lives, his mom more than his dad. It was troubling to watch them forget what they'd already said to you five minutes ago or forget who you were after you just said hello. But we loved them still, and even though it was sometimes uncomfortable, we didn't stay away from them. It just made us feel a little sad and talk in hushed tones among ourselves about what that might mean for us someday. It would be fair to say that most of my siblings and myself have had a nightmare or two regarding this issue.

My father has shown signs of dementia for a few years now. It progresses in spurts, and some times are worse than others. The man you know one day is not the same man you talk to during the next phone call home. Then that new incarnation of my father stays around for a few months, long enough to get comfortable with him, if not entirely satisfied, before he changes again.

About the time I finished the manuscript for my first book, I sent it to my family to read. I knew there would be anger and frustration from some of them because I was airing our dirty laundry. I tried my best to keep the story about me and my own journey, but my story is tangled up in the rest of the people of my family and, inevitably, feelings were hurt by the book. Much like the time I called my father to tell him I was pregnant, I had definite ideas about what his reaction would be to my book. I thought he would be angry. And possibly stop talking to me. Or maybe call and yell at me. I was prepared for all of those things.

I suppose he was hurt and angry initially. He wrote me a letter expressing his embarrassment at having things all written out like that. But then, his mind slipped a little and he was once again a new man whom I didn't know very well. And this man only felt sorrow. Every time I called home over the next year, my father would begin to cry on the phone. He would start telling me that just the other day (even toward the end of that year, to him it was just the other day) he had read my book. And then the crying would get a little harder. He would start to tell me how he thought he had been doing the right thing. How much he loved me and how he thought he was helping me. How I hadn't shown any signs of being hurt and he didn't know he was hurting me, but he wished he would have known, because I was his precious little girl and he would never, ever, ever hurt me on purpose. And by this time, he would be weeping and I would be weeping and my mom would take the phone and we would say our good-byes. It was a year of hell and healing for me, and when his dementia took a stronger hold on him and he forgot about reading the book or that I had written a book at all and even that he had hurt me so much as a child, I never wanted to remind him again. And I won't.

The man I know as my father now is not the man I knew as a child—he's someone new and somewhat different, gentler, kinder, but with the same passionate heart about our Country and his Church.

Now when I see my father, I immediately kiss and hug him. If I see a question in his eyes, him wondering if I already gave him a hug, I do it again immediately. I'm so intensely grateful that I have had these comfortable years of love between us. I ask myself if we would have been given this gift if he didn't have dementia and that question goes unanswered. It seems wrong to be thankful for a disease.

My father, the man who caused me a great deal of pain in

my life, is also an amazing and good man and I love him. And if he forgets how much I love him, I'll remind him as many times as it takes.

Leah Peterson spends her days painting, crafting, writing, and watching reality television reruns. She at one point had seven personalities and wrote a book, Not Otherwise Specified, *that tells her story of becoming integrated. She now has just one personality, and although life is sometimes on the boring side, it's much more manageable. Leah has interviewed many authors and bloggers for video, the Web, and print. You can find her at her website, www.leahpeah.com, and also at www.realmental.org, a site dedicated to talking about and promoting mental health.*

The Best Man

Sarah Brown

Things my father taught me that stuck: How to hit the baseball off the T. All the parts under the hood of my first car. How to appreciate *The Muppet Show*. Never bring home any bikers. That I don't answer to a horn honk: that boy had better come to the door.

My dad is the kind of guy that everyone wants to know. Maybe my dad is the kind of dad that everyone wants as a father. He is quite possibly the tallest, nicest man who ever lived, and if you met him and told me you didn't like him, I'd call you a filthy liar. He runs marathons, and rides roller coasters on his birthday, and washes his car every Saturday whether it needs it or not. He gives sound financial advice and is an excellent dancer and is totally in love with my mom. He sends me e-mails about limericks in the form of a limerick and always has a peppermint in his coat pocket when you need one. He pays $12 a year to subscribe to BlueMountain.com, and sends me Arbor Day e-cards featuring dancing chickens. He once a lost a tooth during a bar fight in Japan while he was in the Navy, but he doesn't like telling that story. When I still lived in my hometown, my dad and I had lunch together every single Wednesday because that was Taco Salad Day at the Presbyterian Church downtown. He likes looking for heads-up pennies on the ground, but when he sees one tails up, he flips it over so it's lucky for the next person who finds it.

My dad is a good man. He is forthright and responsible and honest to an almost annoying degree, refusing to tell the person on the phone that you aren't there if you are. He's also wickedly funny, deadpan, and dry, usually out of the corner of his mouth or under his breath.

My dad is also an extremely patient man. When I was seven years old, I was very excited to join my elementary school T-ball team, only to be suddenly faced with the harsh reality that I had even less athletic ability than was necessary to be a seven-year-old on the T-ball team. I could not hit the ball off the T. My father, undeterred, borrowed the T from my coach, and spent several Saturdays in the backyard with me, trying to teach me basic hand-eye coordination. The neighbors would come outside to laugh and take pictures, and I would get frustrated and yell and pull those dramatic, teeth-gnashing seven-year-old drops to the ground, but my father never lost his cool. Finally, at one of the last games, I not only hit the ball off the T but also hit a home run (due mostly to the fact that the other team couldn't be bothered to stop making daisy chains in the outfield to fetch the ball). The coach presented me with the game ball, signed and dated, and I quit sports while I was ahead. But in my head, I broke the lights and did the slow glory jog like Robert Redford in *The Natural,* and I bet that's how my dad remembers it, too.

When I was twenty-five, and decided I wanted to get in

shape, my dad started running with me by the river three times a week. My father, a marathon runner, never missed a day, sometimes coming to meet me after his own ten-mile run, or workout at the gym. One time he showed up in a polo shirt tucked into khaki pants, with running shoes. When I asked what was with the outfit, he said, "Oh, I'm meeting your mom for a movie afterward," and I said, "Dad, could you at least pretend like you're going to break a sweat here with me?" Of course, he wasn't. While I huffed and puffed, he'd try to start conversations about the Scopes Monkey Trial. When I finished my first mile, he sang the *Rocky* theme.

My dad usually starts his workday by reading *The New York Times* online and sending me links to interesting stories, typically articles about outer space or religion or something, the kind of stuff he and I dork out about together. I can tell that he's having a slow afternoon at the office when I get a link to an obnoxious story from the Vows section, along with the message from sender: "Is this great or what? Talk about a maggot gagger."

I can't decide what I love more—that my dad was bored enough to click on the Vows section, or that lurking somewhere deep inside my financial planner/marathon running/salad for dinner/wash the car every Saturday whether it needs it or not father is a snarky girl.

We then had the following e-mail exchange:

ME: I think there's more to the story than they're letting on. "Nervous preparations with his rambunctious groomsmen."

Like those boys were all blushing and giggling and fainting in the side room like the Bennet sisters.

MY DAD: The Bennet sisters?

ME: From *Pride & Prejudice*?

MY DAD: Oh of course, I remember the series in DC Action Comics, featuring Sergeant Rock of Easy Company, where nothing comes easy.

I called him at this point and said, "So what are you doing, Dad?" and he said, "Eh, reading *Elderhostel* magazine. Someone sent it to me. It's for old people who want to travel or something."

∽

Recently I've had the experience of getting to know each one of my family members one on one, away from home, outside our regular family dynamic, and I've been pleasantly surprised to learn that I like them as people. My dad came to New York by himself to visit me a few years ago, and we had a great time together. We spent an afternoon at the Metropolitan Museum of Art, and came back to Brooklyn too tired to cook dinner. Instead, we stopped at the store for some cheese and fruit and chips and wine, and then sat around my living room, talking and listening to records. We finished one bottle and decided to go back out for another. We talked about old family memories and guys I'd dated and the first time he ever came to New York, back in his twenties. At one point, he asked me to play "At the Zoo" by Simon and Garfunkel. He sang along, closed his eyes, smiled. Then he opened them and said, "Better not tell your mom I fed you chips and wine for dinner."

You know that saying, the best thing a father can do for his children is to love their mother? My father is crazy about my mother. He'll still gaze at her from across the dinner table and interrupt whoever's mid-sentence to say, "Isn't your mom pretty?" They still hold hands and flirt with each other. Once, in high school, they coaxed me into coming out to dinner with them instead of sitting at home on a Saturday night, moping because I'd been dumped. They spent the entire meal playing footsie under the table. They are the first and last couple on the dance floor at weddings and parties. Throughout my entire childhood and teenage years, I never once saw them present anything other than a unified front, and God knows that was not for lack of trying on my part. One of my favorite memories is my father cutting across other runners right before the finish line of one of his races to kiss my mom on the sidelines, everyone clapping and cheering. He dipped her. I took a picture, but I didn't need one. I'd never forget it.

> *One of my favorite memories is my father cutting across other runners right before the finish line of one of his races to kiss my mom on the sidelines, everyone clapping and cheering. He dipped her. I took a picture, but I didn't need one. I'd never forget it.*

My mom told me once that she lost count of the times that people at his company Christmas party would come up to her and tell her, "Your husband is just the nicest man," and she'd say *oh, thanks* and they'd touch her hand and look her in the eye and say, "No. Really. The nicest man. Just treats everybody so *nicely*." My mother also tells the story about the night my dad brought home their first dog, a dachshund named after

Merle Haggard, the runt of the litter, who fit in the pocket of my dad's peacoat. My dad handpicked him, blind in one eye, with a clubfoot. My mother says, "I knew then I'd married the right man."

This is hard to say, because it sounds so corny and maybe borderline weird, but I would be hard pressed to think of another man I think more highly of than my father. He's the best man I know. I usually have to know someone pretty well before I admit that, because I'm afraid they'll think I have a daddy issue. Perhaps my lack of daddy issue is my daddy issue.

He reminds me of Abraham Lincoln and Atticus Finch, all tall and humble and of few words, but the few are witty and wise. Atticus and Abe, but with some Steve Martin thrown in. Right now, I guarantee you my father is reading this and shaking his head, because he is not one for a fuss. What does he think of himself? I don't know. I don't think he spends a lot of time reflecting on this sort of thing. He's not a navel gazer, like his daughter, and I think sometimes it makes him uncomfortable when I heap praise on him. Maybe he thinks if I knew him better, or knew him in his impetuous youth, or remembered his early fathering better, I'd think differently. My dad will tell me over and over again how much he regrets the one time in my life that he spanked me, how he regretted it immediately afterward, he was just tired and cranky and he shouldn't have done it. He tells this story with real remorse in his voice, and it doesn't matter how many times I tell him he really shouldn't worry, because I have absolutely zero memory of it. If you tell my father what a great dad he was when we were growing up, he'll wave his hand and say, "It was your mother who did most of the work."

He is hard on himself. He sets goals and meets them and is troubled when he can't. How else would he be able to run 26 miles in a row without being chased? He's not hard on my brother and me, though—at least not in harsh ways. He taught us both how to drive and how to shake hands and how to manage our money. So far we're both great at driving and handshakes. You'd think that would break the heart of our financial planner father, that neither of his children can really be bothered to balance their checkbook, but we never get any lectures or sermons, just the occasional long sigh. I like to think that means my dad hasn't given up on me yet, that he hopes, just like I do, that one day I'll make a spreadsheet and stick to it, because currently my monthly budgets are not so much numbers on spreadsheets, but shimmery ideas that flit around inside my head like baby unicorns. Maybe one day my dad will ask me a question about my 401(k) or Roth IRA and I'll say something other than, "Yes, eleventeen. Negative three. Colorado."

Maybe my dad knows that one day I'll wake up and it will be the day I decide to make and follow a budget, just like how I finally managed to hit the ball off the T. Or maybe I just like to tell myself my dad knows these things, when in reality, he's crossing his fingers but resigning himself to my debtors'-prison fate right along with me.

In all honesty, the worst thing I can imagine is disappointing my father. Sometimes I tear up just thinking about it. I guess that's a daddy issue on some level but, as they go, not really a bad one to have. Because he's never made me feel like I've disappointed him, and in the past thirty years, I've made some colossal mistakes. He sighs a lot, and purses his lips, and I've received more than a few much-deserved talking-tos, but he never raises his voice.

So, are you sick of hearing about how great my dad is yet? Yeah, there's the thing. The thing with my dad is that there is no thing with my dad. I have no repressed anger, no issue to talk out with a therapist. There's no weird hang-up or anything; I just really like and respect him. We get along. We speak the same language. We laugh at the same things. If I weren't related to him, I'd still hang out with him. We'd be friends.

I know, I know. Now try dating me.

There's this story I've read in celebrity magazines over and over again, where Gwyneth Paltrow tells how her father took her to Paris for the first time when she was a little girl, just the two of them, so that she'd always remember the first time she was in Paris was with a man who would love her forever. I imagine the point of this story is to be sweet and heartwarming, but it kind of skeeves me out. No matter how great he is, a woman can't express too much love for her dad without sounding a little icky. Anytime I start talking about my father, I wonder in the back of my head, *Am I being Gwyneth Paltrow in Paris right now?*

When I first meet a guy, and we have those preliminary trading-stories-about-our-families conversations, I catch myself holding back with my dad stories, because I don't want to sound like a weirdo who thinks her dad is so awesome. Eventually, all the dad stories come out, only I manage to drop them casually, piece by piece, so no one is overwhelmed with disbelief that my dad could be this cool. And then the weird thing happens: The guy becomes interested in my dad. If he hasn't already met him, he asks if he can. Nearly every male friend I have has at one point exclaimed, "Man! Your dad is so cool!" My friend Roy and I entered into a bet once, and if I won, he had to take me for lunch at the Four Seasons, followed by a helicopter ride. If he won, he decided his prize was that I would have to fly my father into town for a weekend of hanging out.

My college boyfriend once told me that his greatest fear was that at some point in our relationship, he'd screw up somehow, and my father would take him aside and "speak very sternly and directly" to him. Of course that never happened, but he has no idea how lucky he was. My dad liked him. My high school boyfriends, not so much. They were all scared of him, and he took advantage of that, thoroughly enjoying putting the fear of God into them as often as he could.

In high school, when a boy would call and my dad happened to answer, he'd yell upstairs, without even covering the receiver, "Sarah! There's some mouth breather on the phone for you!" When my first boyfriend drove me to our first formal dance, and all the parents were taking pictures beforehand, my dad pulled my boyfriend aside, put his hand on his shoulder, and said, "Andy, keep your eyes on the road and your hands on the wheel." And it worked. That kid was too scared to slow dance. Even after Andy had been around for a while and felt more comfortable with my family, my dad liked to keep him on his toes. Once my dad took us out to the all-you-can-eat Chinese buffet, and Andy came with us. We had a fun meal, everyone laughing and talking, but when the bill came, my dad grew quiet, studied it for a minute, and then leaned forward and said, "Andy, how many times did you go back to the buffet, son?"

I dated another boy in high school, one that my father couldn't stand. My dad was suspicious of everything this guy did, especially his golfing habits. Apparently he let it be known once that he spent an afternoon golfing alone, and this was unfathomable to my father—some kind of weird final straw. "Who golfs alone?!" he'd demand. "Weirdos."

The boy was oblivious to my father's scorn, however, and a few weeks after he unceremoniously dumped me on my birthday, I ran into him at a party. I hadn't seen him in a while; I hoped I looked good. I said hello nonchalantly.

He asked about my dad.

"I saw him the other day, at the gas station," he told me. "I mean, we didn't talk or anything, but I kind of feel like we didn't have to. I feel like your dad and I understand each other."

∽

Last Saturday evening, while I was getting ready to go meet some friends for dinner, my phone rang, and it said "Home," so I assumed it was my mother, because my father is not much for the telephone.

Our phone conversations are typically about things like how Miss Piggy would have made a great Lady Macbeth. I'll call home to talk to my parents, and my mom will tell me about her garden's progress and what my brother is doing, and ask me if I've done my taxes and renewed my license yet, and then she'll hand the phone to my dad and he'll say, "It's a real shame that the Muppets didn't ever do any Shakespeare, like *Hamlet*. That would've been funny, to do *Hamlet* with some pigs." Then he's like, "Oh, hold on: your mom wants to talk again."

But anyway, last Saturday night, I answered, and my dad said, "Hello!" in this smiley, relaxed voice, and I said, "Well, hello!" and we had a pleasant little conversation about nothing. Then, right before we got off the phone, he said, "Do you re-member—you probably don't remember this—but when you were little, and every Saturday night at five-thirty you and I would watch *The Muppet Show* together?" And immediately my eyes filled up with tears and I was like, oh man, don't do this to me now! Because of course I remember that. My mom would be getting ready for them to go out, but my dad would already be dressed, and before the babysitter arrived, he and I would sit on the couch together and watch Kermit. I will for-ever associate the Muppets with my dad. I'm not one of those girls who plans out her wedding, but I've always known that when I get married, the song I'll dance to with my dad will be "The Rainbow Connection."

I may be unsure of my situation, but my father does have some father issues of his own. His own dad was a gruff, grumpy man of even fewer words, and not many of them kind. My dad doesn't ever remember his own father telling him he loved him, or that he was proud of him, so he made it a point to say it to my brother and me every time we said goodbye. He'd put his hand on your shoulder, look you in the eye, and say, "Sarah, I love you and I'm proud of you." My brother and I, being the sarcastic children that we are, perhaps felt a little too showered with sincerity by this, and started saying it back to him as a joke. My mom told me this hurt his feelings, so he's stopped. I wish he'd start again. Now I get what he meant: everyone should hear that from his or her parents. It seeps in after a while. You start to believe it.

Sarah Brown is the host and creator of the Cringe Reading Series, and the editor of Cringe: Teenage Diaries, Journals, Notes, Letters, Poems, and Abandoned Rock Operas *(Crown, 2008). She has blogged at her Web site, queserasera.org, since 2001. She was born in Tulsa, Oklahoma, and lives in Brooklyn, New York.*

Adam and Red

Eden Marriott Kennedy

I met Babs, my future mother-in-law, and her third husband, Red, outside their four-bedroom Mediterranean in Palm Springs on a warm June evening in 1995. I guess they'd heard us pull up in my dinky Toyota because they were on the sidewalk before Jack and I were even out of the car.

My first impression was that Jack's mom, blond and broad-faced and stout, bore shockingly little resemblance to her son.* Jack's stepfather, Red, stepped up to give me a skeptical hello and take my overnight bag. If anything, Jack resembled *him* more; after years of raising Barbara's sons, Red had imprinted a fair amount of Brooklyn Jew on two wild Irish boys from Rego Park, Queens.

Barbara was perfectly warm and welcoming to me, and in the twelve years since that first evening, her conduct toward me has never changed. Red, however. Maybe he was feeling a little protective of Jack, being that Jack's wife had recently ex-

*We should try to pardon casting agents who cobble together whole TV sitcom families using actors whose only similarity to each other is that they belong to the same gym.

cused herself from the marriage and here I was, a little too soon for him to get excited about? This weekend was not really about showing me off like some sort of consolation prize. Though Red's hair was fading from copper to gray, as he hugged Jack, he looked nothing like a man who was beginning to die of lung cancer.

Babs had called Jack a week earlier to break the news, and Jack's reaction to the diagnosis had been dry and typical. He hung up the phone and said to me, "Red's got cancer. Chemo starts in two weeks. Well, now we have an excuse to buy him some cool hats."

Jack never uses the word "cool"; his vocabulary is far more colorful than that. He probably said "stylin'" or "dope" or "swish" or another word I can't recall because this exchange took place twelve years ago, though I can still see him standing in my apartment with his hand on my dark green Trimline phone, perhaps imagining Red with a fresh Yankees hat rolled up and tucked into his back pocket.

I dropped into Jack's life at a singularly absorbing time. In the sense that it completely absorbed me: I all but forget who I was on and off for that first year. Jack's wife had left him months earlier (for reasons that seemed simple yet, to him, mystifying) but divorce was still theoretical. There were echoes of her everywhere—in a note from one of Jack's sisters addressed to "Mr. and Mrs. Kennedy," still under a magnet on his refrigerator; in a copy of *Penthouse* he'd hidden behind *Women Who Run with the Wolves*—though Jack did his best to mute them. I had just left a long-ish relationship myself and hadn't really wanted to drop into a new one so quickly, but I had a competitive instinct—I wanted to win Jack away from the

woman who'd dropped his heart on the floor. I also felt that familiar need to fix a guy's life for him.

We began the long summer by alternating weekends of
drunken record parties at my apartment with weekends in the
baking hot desert, watching Barbara care for a steadily degen-
erating man who, despite recalculating for terminal illness, still
didn't appear to like me very much.

So I would retreat from the family nucleus, put on the
green plaid bikini I'd purchased at Jack's insistence to replace
my old Speedo tank, and retire to an inflatable raft in his
mom's warm little backyard pool. In the evenings, Jack and I
would borrow Red's Cadillac and drive to the big grocery
store in Palm Desert where all the gold lamé widows shopped,
and then Jack would rustle up something elegant—basil-
encrusted salmon, or veal osso bucco, or New Zealand green-
lipped mussels vinaigrette. Jack's work in the kitchen was
meant to tempt Red's chemo-wrecked appetite, but a side
benefit appeared as he found a way to my heart through my
stomach, and I found a way to his mother's by washing the
dishes afterward.

No one seemed to notice that I was using a dying man's last
months with his family as a series of romantic, catered weekend getaways.

When I did try to talk to Red, it often ended badly. Once
when I was drying myself off after a dip in the pool, Jack
wheeled Red out on the hot patio, probably to thaw him out
(someone was always turning up the air-conditioning), and I
casually asked Red about how much he used to smoke. Because
I'm *really tactful*.

Red gave me a quick rundown of his career as a cosmetics

executive in New York, tense meetings with Max Factor or Charles Revson, hectic conferences and hours on the phone when he'd have three cigarettes burning at once—he kept forgetting he already had one burning so he'd light another and then another and then smoke them all down to the nub. As he told me this, he looked terribly defeated and I realized that I was a complete jerk for reminding him what he'd done to invite this illness, so I went back inside the house to shoot myself. Then I made lunch, leaving Red marooned on the patio in his wheelchair, thinking about his sins.

Eventually Red's hair was coming out in tufts, so one night after dinner Jack handed me a Norelco clipper—I'd been buzz-cutting Jack's hair all summer and felt comfortable wielding the instruments of barberdom—and told me it was time. Red was stoic about it, and I silently sheared off what was left on his scalp, terrified of nicking his fragile skin. When I was done, he rubbed his head with his hands and gave me a short smile. So that was something.

Another time Jack found me goofing off with a book of *L.A. Times* crosswords out on the patio and he said, "You know, Red did the *New York Times* crossword in pen every day for years. Why don't you do a puzzle together?" I rearranged myself so Red could look over my shoulder. Chemo-induced neuropathy had numbed his fingers until he couldn't hold a pen, but he was still sharp enough to dictate most of the right answers to me, all the while complaining about how simple-minded the *L.A. Times* puzzle editor was.

Though lunch was always casual—cold cuts or hot dogs and potato chips on paper plates, always plenty of beer and Diet Coke, suit yourself—dinner would take place at the large, oblong oak dining table under a slowly rotating fan with a table-cloth and nice wine, everyone barefoot and still in bathing suits or shorts. Jack would wheel Red to the table and aperitifs would kick off with a bang.

"BARBARA, I'M SO COLD, TURN THE AIR-CONDITIONING OFF!"

"THERE ARE OTHER PEOPLE IN THIS HOUSE BESIDES YOU, WE HAVE TO KEEP IT COMFORT-ABLE FOR EVERYONE."

"BUT I'M ILL, BARBARA!"

"DON'T BE SO SELFISH, WHAT ABOUT THE REST OF US?"

Exchanges like this unnerved me until Jack explained that arguing loudly was a priority in Babs's and Red's relationship. When Jack was a teenager, he could always tell when they'd had a really big fight because he'd come home at night and Red would be trying to calm himself down by scrubbing the kitchen floor in his underwear.

Compromises would be made, tempers would cool, and we'd sit down together to pass the peas. As the summer progressed and Red was less inclined to politely face a dinner he had no intention of eating, he would stay in bed and rest and Barbara would feel free to hold forth, and the subject she really warmed to was her first marriage, to Adam, Jack's dad.

The tales that poured forth got more Byzantine with each subsequent bottle of wine. It depended on Barbara's mood how she'd approach a story about Adam; the facts seldom changed, and her preferred form was long, detailed, and nuanced, but the spin could vary from week to week.

The basic facts: Babs had met Adam on a photo shoot—

they were both working as models in New York City. It was the early fifties, and Barbara, who had been a dancer at the Copacabana, could easily be mistaken for Grace Kelly. Adam was fifteen years older, a rugged but polished Midwestern type who'd worked in the art department of *Esquire* magazine before turning to acting. Their attraction was immediate and intense. Babs was nineteen years old when they married. They moved to California and had their first son, Regan, when Babs was twenty, and then Jack when she was twenty-two. They moved to Malibu. Adam started writing treatments and screenplays. For a variety of reasons, things began to fall apart. She took the boys back to New York. Adam followed. One memorable afternoon he tried to reconcile with her. "The sex wasn't that good," Barbara said, shrugging.

Six weeks later we were at the dining room table and she was gearing up to tell the story again, which Jack took as his cue to go to bed early and leave me with half a bottle of Martel. So I stayed up with Barbara and listened as the story became more detailed. Early in their marriage they were living in Malibu, and Adam would leave Barbara every morning at the same time to go to his rented office to write for Hollywood. "He'd take the car and leave me stranded, miles from anything, with two small children!" Her indignation, forty years after the fact, was still vivid. Adam's behavior in general rankled her: He never helped with the children, and in general behaved like a man entitled to be served; they disagreed about nearly everything; his mother was difficult to please; he may or may not have been having affairs. Eventually Barbara threw up her hands and moved back to New York with the boys so she could work as a model again and start over. Adam followed them east but Babs would have none of it. He persisted; he said he loved her, he wanted to be with the boys. She hired a woman to help with Regan and Jack while she worked. One day while the children were at the park, Adam arrived at her apartment with flowers. "The sex was good," she said with a dismissive flip of her hand, "but the marriage was over."

The Martel gone, I poured myself into bed. It was brutally bright when I got up five hours later, the day already sticky and hot. I shuffled out to the patio, where Jack was in his shorts, drinking coffee and reading the *L.A. Times* sports section.

"Just had to stay up and have one more drink."

I flipped him the bird.

"I love it when you talk to me like that. Let's try again. Coffee? Brain transplant?"

Barbara slid open the patio screen door. "Good morning, darlings. How did everyone sleep?"

"I slept great, but Eden looks like she could use a Bloody Mary."

"Ooh, a Bloody Mary sounds fabulous, would you like one, dear?"

I held my head in my hands. "No, thank you. Maybe if you have some Advil?"

"Of course, darling! Just go into my medicine cabinet, there's aspirin, ibuprofen, whatever you want, help yourself. I'm going to check on the laundry."

When she was gone, Jack said, "You know, back in the day, she was famous for being able to drink guys—hard guys—under the table."

I was afraid that if I moved, my head would fall off and roll right into the pool.

Jack told me to go get some Advil and he'd get me a glass of water. So I got up and tiptoed past a sleeping Red and into the master bath, where I opened the medicine cabinet, and there, on a glass shelf next to a container of Tums, sat a sweaty tumbler of vodka on the rocks on a wet cocktail napkin.

> *I opened the medicine cabinet and there, on a glass shelf next to a container of Tums, sat a sweaty tumbler of vodka on the rocks on a wet cocktail napkin.*

I reacted in the only way I could think to at the time: in complete denial. I found the Tylenol, took out two caplets, replaced the bottle, and shut the cabinet door.

Back out on the patio, Barbara and Jack were chatting. I sat down, hiding the Tylenol in my fist. "Did you get any aspirin, darling?" asked Babs.

"Uh, no, I forgot," I said, afraid to admit what I'd found in her bathroom.

"Sit there, I'll get some for you," she said, getting up.

Jack handed me a glass of iced water and said, "You can't be that hungover. What, you forgot what you went in there for?"

I showed him the Tylenol and then told him about the drink chilling in the medicine cabinet. I'd never seen him so delighted. "Now *that's* hangover maintenance," he said. "Take a tip from a pro. Too bad we don't have any more of those pot brownies."

The weekend before, when I'd stayed up in Santa Barbara— nobody'd been able to take over my Saturday shift at the bookstore—a friend of Barbara's had brought Red a plate of

brownies into which he'd baked a handful of marijuana. It was
the happiest Red had been in months, according to Jack, hint-
ing at a portion of Red's past life I hadn't heard about yet:
Madison Avenue stoner.

God bless him.

Later, I put back those first two Tylenol. It seemed like a
waste to throw them away just because they'd been in my
sweaty hand for twenty minutes.

Down in the desert, summer turned into fall in name only;
the temperature was still in the nineties most days. By that time
Jack's brother, Regan, had flown in from New York to be a
full-time nurse for Red, and Jack's sisters (from Red and
Barbara's marriage) rotated through when they could. Kate,
who was ten years younger than Jack, had just had her second
child, a daughter they photographed in bed next to Red, two
bald heads napping together. Maryann, one year younger than
Kate, flew in from Paris, where she'd been working as a tour
guide and studying Raymond Chandler at the Sorbonne.

At the end of her stay in Palm Springs, Maryann was reluctant to leave her father and return to school.

"Go," said Red, who for Maryann's sake was faking normalcy by appearing at the dinner table. He popped a whole
Ding Dong into his mouth as though it was part of his cure.
"Look, I'm eating! I'll get through this. Go back to Paris, we'll
see you at Christmas."

She went, but six weeks later she was flying back home for
Red's funeral.

I had managed the Sunday night shift, so after counting the

cash drawers and locking up at 11:30 P.M., I bought two Diet
Cokes at a gas station and started the three-hour drive down to
Palm Springs. I received a speeding ticket from a potbellied
lady cop outside Tarzana around 12:15 A.M., and suffered a
late-night ramp closure on I-10 that rerouted me through the
parking lot of an abandoned truck stop, where I felt sure an
enterprising gang of Bill and Ted lookalikes from San Dimas
would be luring disoriented drivers into a magical, time-
traveling phone booth, but nothing like that happened.

The house was dark when I got there; I rang the bell and then
followed a groggy Jack into Red's dusty office, and watched
him lie down and fall asleep in the middle of a queen-sized air
mattress that lay on the floor. Maybe one Diet Coke would
have been enough, for when I squeezed in next to Jack and
tried to will myself into metabolizing the remaining 80 grams
of caffeine, pretty much nothing happened. I finally lost my
grip on consciousness around 5:00 A.M., but was roused at 7:30
by Jack's absence and the smell of French roast.

I found Barbara still in her robe, pink-eyed and watching
Good Morning America with the sound off, lying in the bed that
Red had died in. I crawled in next to her. She laughed and
hugged me and then wiped her nose with a crumpled tissue.
"Who am I going to fight with now?" she said.

The funeral was at a military cemetery in Riverside, an
hour away. Red, who had once been a driver for General
Patton, hadn't left a will, but Barbara knew he'd wanted a military burial. Regan hadn't brought a decent jacket with him
from New York, so he borrowed one of Jack's and the two of
them drove off to the cemetery together in the white Ford F-150
work truck that Red had bought for Jack in thanks for his help

in Red's final days. Barbara, Maryann, and Kate took a rented limo, and I followed, sweaty and alone in my un-air-conditioned car, imagining Red looking down in a pair of ugly plaid golf pants and a straw stingy-brim with a faded hatband, nodding his grudging approval of me from the ankle-obscuring fog of the afterlife.

Jack said a few shaky words over the coffin and then read a poem that they'd found in Red's desk. The rabbi who spoke hadn't known Red at all, and for some reason his wooden, clueless benedictions tipped me over the edge. Exhausted, I cried—deep, wracking sobs that made Maryann, herself completely miserable, cling to my arm.

Everyone else was headed back to Babs's house, but Jack and I didn't have the luxury to mourn with them—we had an appointment to look at an apartment in L.A. in less than two hours. We had decided to move in together (someday his divorce would come through) and pursue new careers. Jack would be getting his contractor's license and I'd be using a connection I'd made in film school to become an apprentice editor in a small firm that cut trailers and TV spots. We signed the lease for our new apartment that afternoon still wearing our funeral clothes.

It was a hard winter. The big money that Jack was promised he'd be making hadn't come through; we burned through my savings and were making ends meet with my $300-a-week job (itself a daily minefield of small humiliations and huge egos) and an overtaxed credit card. Our cats didn't like each other. Someone kept flinging used diapers up onto the roof of the building across the way.

By March the financial rope we were dangling from was

frayed beyond repair, so in the interest of taking a cheap mental health weekend, we used the last of the credit I had left on my Visa to buy two airplane tickets to Phoenix. Jack's divorce had finally gone through, we were about to get hitched, and it was time to introduce me to Jack's father, Adam, and his wife of twenty-five years, Susan.

Never mind that I got a flat on the way home from work that day—a Turkish mechanic got my tire patched and put me back on the road in twenty minutes.

Never mind that halfway to the airport Jack realized that he'd forgotten to bring the index card on which he'd written their phone number and address—Adam and Susan were unlisted, and because they weren't picking us up at the airport, we had no way of knowing where to tell a cab to go, so we had to turn around in L.A. rush-hour traffic and go back to get it.

Never mind that the horrible woman at Southwest Airlines treated me like a moron for missing our original flight on a busy Friday night, and then pretended there were no seats until the next day until her suspicious coworker leaned over and pointed out that there were two seats on the next flight, if we hurried.

Never mind that I hadn't had anything to eat since a tuna sandwich at lunch and had to make dinner out of a foil pack of peanuts on the plane.

No, I wasn't about to break down or give up. I held it together in my grubby shirt and jeans while shaking Adam's and Susan's hands for the first time, finally understanding how worldly and cultured they were, and aware that their first impression of me wasn't measuring up to Jack's adored and stylish ex-wife. I kept my cool during cocktails when Adam tested my social dexterity by changing the subject to orgasms. I made it through separate beds and tall drinks at lunch the next day and a Cactus League baseball game to which I'd unadvisedly worn a too-young-for-me miniskirt and some cute but ill-fitting zebra-striped clogs that made me walk like a pigeon-toed geisha. When Susan handed me a cold ballpark hot dog, I ate it without complaint. And I didn't panic when Jack disappeared with his dad Sunday morning and left me with nothing but a distracted Susan and an abiding need to disappear into the funny papers.

After Jack came back from breakfast with Adam, he took me for a walk by the golf course and told me that he'd spilled all our problems out to his father, who'd recommended that we cut our losses and move back up to Santa Barbara. "What do you think?" he asked. My response was to start crying uncontrollably.

All the stress of the past year, of watching Red die and precipitating Jack's divorce and moving with new hope to a new city and watching my future fall apart—being horribly in debt and drinking too much and working until 1:00 A.M. at a low-level job and if I quit it what would I do with my life, I was thirty-two years old, how many more times could I start over and find a new career and make a success of myself? I hated Santa Barbara, but if I wanted to stay with Jack, I'd have to go back. I couldn't embrace such a cruel sacrifice.

I was falling apart and I couldn't get up.

I couldn't stop crying. I may have been hysterical. No one knew what to do with me. Jack was patient and kind, but when he ran out of ideas, he sent Susan in to see if there was anything she could do—"Now's your chance to be a mom," he told her. Adam stayed in the living room; he was expecting an old friend to come by, his former English professor from DePauw whom they'd invited for dinner. "He's a lovely man," said Susan, trying. I sobbed; I'd gotten a C in college English.

I didn't make it out to the table for dinner that night, and in the morning I ate toast as cheerfully as I could manage, my eyes swollen, my heart full of shame. Adam spent the morning talking with Jack and giving me a wide berth. Susan drove us to the airport in silence.

Adam and Susan declined the invitation to our backyard wedding in Santa Barbara six months later. I don't remember what reason they gave, I just assumed that they felt like Jack was rushing into marriage number two with an emotional basket case and it wasn't going to last so why waste good money on airfare? I wasn't offended; I pretty much felt like I deserved it.

"I wish Red was here," said Jack.

"We all do," said Barbara.

"Your kitchen floor will never be that clean again," said Jack.

Barbara laughed. "When Red was done, you could have *eaten* off that floor."

We toasted. "To Red."

A year later at their condo in Connecticut, Adam had a heart attack and died in his reading chair while Susan was running errands in town. The UPS man saw Adam through the window and tapped on the door, but assumed he was sleeping and left his package on the stoop.

That disastrous weekend in Phoenix ended up being the only time I ever spent with Adam. At his funeral I both laughed and cried more than I would have predicted for a man with whom I felt almost no connection but whose family I was growing to love.

I'm pleased to say that over the course of time I've developed a nice relationship with Susan. She's often expressed regret that Adam did not live long enough to meet his grandson, Jackson, a funny boy who likes to send her watercolors in the mail, which she puts on her refrigerator with magnets and admires every day.

So that's two grandpas that never got to meet our boy, and two fathers-in-law who went to their graves thinking I was not the brightest bulb on the Hanukkah bush.

A funny thing happened on the first anniversary of Adam's death. I was sitting at my computer at work—contrary to expectation, I did manage to find a job I liked in Santa Barbara—and just for a minute I felt like he was standing behind me, looking over my shoulder and reading a little article I was writing about Greece with approval.

I'm prone to listening for ghosts, I know. But when the opportunity to reach out in life has gone, it's a comfort to imagine securing a small measure of goodwill in death.

Eden Marriott Kennedy has been blogging at fussy.org since 2001 and during that time has covered everything from giving birth in her

bathroom to the daily growth of her own hair. A mother, wife, and yoga nerd, she can also be found at yogabeans.com, "your internet source for plastic action figures demonstrating Ashtanga yoga." She's been featured in The San Francisco Chronicle, The New York Times, *and* The Santa Barbara Independent, *and has blogged (about* Nova *and* Nature*) for PBS. She lives in Southern California.*

Circular Plug

Gail Armstrong

After years of denial, but now actively bullied by her friends, our mother agrees to call our father on his affair. One weekend, while he's off again with his mistress at the Montreal Ritz, Mom goes to stay at a friend's house. As instructed, she leaves behind a note saying, "I've left. Do not come after me." Then adds: "Should you want to talk, I'll be at M's." Arriving back late Sunday night, Dad finds the note. He has a few drinks, then goes to bed.

Late Monday morning, he calls her. She confronts him about his mistress—only the latest in a steady string over the past 10 years, but they won't ever talk about that—saying either stop or their marriage is through. He takes a slug of scotch. Inhales, exhales. "Well, if that's what you want," he says, then hangs up.

Then he's on the phone to his children. He calls me at work. I'm seventeen, but have already left home, going to high school in the morning, and waitressing the rest of the day and on weekends. He asks me to make my way up Yonge Street until I run into him. We find each other about a block away from the avenue where my childhood was spent, from the same old house where he's still living, and which is still the dark mazy diorama of so many of my dreams.

He's drunk and dazed, slow and heavy stepping under a cloak of sorrow and guilty relief. I know what he's about to say; it's been a long time coming. "Your mother has left me." And he needs and we want him to be the good guy—years of family mythology are hard to shake—but still I'm glad to hear his voice catch on the words; it stops me from saying brutal obvious things. He tells me how sad and he's feeling so lone—, then pauses, aware that the crowd's not rooting enough for the home team. I don't want to cry, only kick him in the shins, but he takes me in his arms and whispers, "Oh, sweetie, couldn't you at least act surprised?"

Then I cry. Then he turns and is gone, and I go back to work.

My father was born into one of those quintessential upper-middle-class WASP families, the kind that turn gorgeous young leads in romantic comedies into clumsy, stuttering odes to self-doubt—every inch of their future in-laws' home and demeanor emanating the self-evidence that they will never, God forbid, be good enough to join the Club.

Despite having no qualms with the specious social views of his class, merely having a bit of an artistic bent was enough to have my father branded the most eccentric child of the family. With Coke-bottle glasses and a clumsy gait, he fumbled his way through elementary school—his early mornings spent in the bathroom crying and pleading with his dad through the shower curtain to let him stay home, please, just today. Still he went, failed a grade, fell ill, and slumped to the optometrist's every few months—dazzled each time he stepped out into the street by the blurs transformed temporarily into bright signs and clear throngs. *And oh,* he says, *although they didn't think much of me at the time, I sure did like the ladies.* I wonder whether he already knew that women would be the bane and guilty thrill of his life.

In grade seven he transferred to a staunch private school in the heart of Toronto, left his geek self behind him, and suddenly came into his own. He began to paint, built sets for school plays, puppets, and theaters—selling tickets to the neighborhood kids for the shows he put on in his garage—and pulley devices to glide him from upstairs windows down to the lawn. He collected butterflies, mounted and framed them—conjuring up the heartbreaking image of a bespectacled, big-toothed boy tiptoeing through summer camp with his butterfly net, stopping wild-eyed behind a bush to whisper, "Oh, golly, *Ancyloxypha numitor!*"—brawny boys in the background, sweaty with wrestling and deer-stalking archery. But when I tease him about it, he says, "Well, you know, that is when I realized you could be true to yourself and still get along."

In the chipped and faded grandeur of my grandmother's house I tread lightly

Dad's mother was nicknamed Queenie for no hidden reason—a spoiled and effortlessly callous woman for whom there was no mystery over where the center of the universe lay. Her only two disappointments in life were (1) not having a daughter—for which she compensated by dressing her two youngest sons up as girls and letting their hair grow to long curls for the first two years of their life and (2) not having been a member of the British aristocracy—this only mildly offset by befriending a duchess or two, one of whom got her antique lace dress peed upon by Granny's dog, a three-legged toy poodle named Jaunty, and reminiscing about her one long-ago dinner with the Queen, usually omitting the presence of the hundred other people who also attended.

Dinner with Queenie was reliably terrifying, as she'd sit at the head of the table, yardstick in hand, poised to rap the knuckles of hands that reached for the wrong silverware. Peas had to be pushed onto the fork from the front, not the side, and never more than three at a time; ice cream on cones bitten and chewed, as only the lower class licked; the Union Jack hoisted on the flagpole early in the morning, lowered and folded just so at dusk; swimming a hushed and splashless affair. Any deviation from the King's English was fiercely admonished, and because it was unacceptable that we miss Sunday school when in the country, summer services were held in the barn. Queenie reminisced often of her travels to exotic lands, though many of her forays abroad appeared to consist chiefly of complaining to the staff in four-star hotels (shocked at the sight of a futon in their room in Kyoto, she called down to insist that a "real" bed be brought up) and sending harassed drivers off to buy rugs in the Kasbah.

I was told by a childhood friend of my father's that when he'd been a boy, instead of the bogeyman, mothers would threaten to send their sons to my grandmother's house if they didn't behave.

After trotting the globe and indulging her every whim for

seven decades, Queenie lay down and continued to reign from bed for the last twenty-four years of her life. Head propped on mounds of silk cushions, silver bell by her side, she ran roughshod over the "help" that she hired and fired at a truly remarkable rate—continually lamenting their inability to slice the zucchini correctly (circles not strips), to distinguish the good from the everyday china, and to be white of skin—and reproached her three grown sons for not calling daily. When not threatening to change her will or excommunicating a now-former daughter-in-law, she spent the time discovering the real world through daytime TV, which informed her that homosexuality had been invented, unmarried people were having sex with abandon (and each other), and all kids were whacked out on drugs. Despite overwhelming signs that the times were changing, she refused to believe that it was more than a grubby passing phase, and nothing ever came to shake her belief in her superiority, the laziness of the poor, or the subhumanness of those she employed. Her idea of a concession on the issue of race was to state that, after much thought, she'd decided that, though marriage was naturally out of the question, "I would be less offended were you to frequent a colored man than a Jew."

Our very last visit before she died was the only time she ever brought up the subject of my adoption. "What is it like knowing you are not one of us?," she wanted to know.

An impostor.

Breaking with family traditions, my father went west to study painting and soon became enthralled by architecture.

After graduating with honors in Toronto—thanks in part to a fine thesis made dazzling by his father's secretary—he went to work in Boston, where he is glad to report that he was regularly rebuked for his after-hours activities. The party animal was born. Six months later, he hightailed it out of the States to avoid being drafted to Korea, and made his way to London, where he helped in the city's postwar reconstruction—sharing a flat in Notting Hill with a throng of fellow expats and a six-foot-five future Anglican minister who slept in the tub. There he met and fell in love with a beautiful Australian girl who was working as a model. It was his first true love affair. My parents' versions of how the courtship went diverge on major details, my father having forgotten that his girl was being actively pursued by other men, and that he had to work hard to change her mind about him being "a pleasant but rather odd-looking young man."

Though inevitable that 25 years of marriage and a not-amicable divorce taints one's view of things, what strikes me most about both versions of this love story is that *passion* never seems to have entered into it. There were weekends away in separate rooms, sometimes with family members in tow, much moving in the same crowd, and an only gradual realization that "he was a kind, reliable man" and "we'd grown very fond of each other." So instead of going home to Australia, my mother moved to Canada, where they wed in bitter cold January, their honeymoon spent in a country house—after a long slippery drive down ice-clad roads, stopping to fit chains on tires in the blizzard—with nothing but eggs to eat for a week. My mother had never seen snow before, and has spent the rest of her life trying to avoid it.

With every passing year
I lose the social graces that terrified my childhood.

Their honeymoon years were gay times of hard work—quick changing the bedroom into an office when clients came by; bed shunted out back and tables installed, with my mother made secretary for the hour (aside from which she had been forbidden by Queenie to work, though "I shall allow you to volunteer. May I suggest the Junior League?").

There were long trips overseas, sometimes for months at a stretch, nannies and housekeepers, extra uniformed help for the many cocktail and dinner parties. They had an astonishing number of friends and a great fondness for conga lines, Post Office, and Pass the Orange, whoops of laughter, and stealing kisses that we watched through the rails of the banister. Consuming gallons of booze seemed perfectly normal at the time: martini lunches, cocktails, wine at the table, and after-dinner drinks, all made acceptable by having a name. As long as there was a set time of day when drinking could commence, there was never any thought of alcoholism—despite much clock-watching going on starting at 4:30 P.M. Weekends and holidays were even better as the shaker could be shaken at noon.

He tells the same five lame jokes at the dinner table for fifteen
years, reveling in the groans that get louder each time. He smokes a
pipe and wears apricot neckerchiefs. He grows a beard, which causes
weeks of dissent so, one night at dinner, he comes to the table with
the left half shaven off so: "See, now everyone's happy."

∾

> *Like most people, my memories of girlhood are selective and no doubt self-serving—as we pick and choose those that best help shape our image, salt our wounds, justify our foibles and occasionally lousy disposition.*

Like most people, I expect, my memories of girlhood are selective and no doubt self-serving—as we pick and choose those that best help shape our image, salt our wounds, justify our foibles and occasionally lousy disposition. And I realize that I don't have many memories of my father alone because, like most dads of the day, he wasn't really around. As he tells it, only once did he take care of us three on his own—an event so trying he made sure never to repeat it. He remained a remote figure, a center unyielding around which moved his wife and children, our minds forced into isolation by his presence. But he was revered by all, associated mostly with report-card scrutiny, the much-touted redemption of hard manual labor, lining up for spankings when he got home, laughter and playing games of his own invention. *Pikapolka* was the finest of all, with Dad as a ravenous monster chasing us round the house, roaring *watch out,* he was closing in, till he'd catch you, pin you down, pull up your shirt, and gobble your belly, shouting out for "More ketchup! More salt! Bring it now! Yum yum!" till you almost passed out from laughing.

When all three children were young, we spent most of our summers at The Farm: a few hundred acres north of the city with tennis court, swimming pools, ponds stocked with trout, and where the closest thing to livestock were the poodles. On either side were real farms and true farmers, with cattle and chickens and 4-H Club members, unstintingly selfless when we uppity city folk got stuck in the mud or snow.

In the middle of the property sat my grandparents' handsome brick farmhouse, surrounded over the hills by a newly built home for each of their three sons and families. Ours was The Cabin (the imaginative naming of things was clearly not a strong suit), the coziest and smallest of all with a perpetual divine smell of wood, mothballs, the smoke of last night's fire, chlorine on beach towels, and raspberry tarts from the town bakery. There were faces in the knots of the wooden rafters, turning evil as the sun went down and the wolves began to howl in the woods. Deer, groundhogs, tadpoles, turtles, and snakes; skunks and porcupines requiring great stocks of tomato juice and two trips to the vet each year. There was a beaver dam in the river that cut through the forest, thick morning dew and dandelions beheaded between the toes, picnics and forts, great armies formed and battles waged between all the ten-star generals, truth or dare and older cousins who awed us with their knowledge and told dirty jokes I didn't understand but laughed like they were the funniest things ever (and perhaps made the mistake of repeating them to my mother), burping, distance-peeing, and watermelon seed–spitting contests. All ours once chores at home and for Queenie had been done.

My father would drive up from the city for weekends, and late Friday afternoons I would head down the dirt road to meet him. There was no fixed meeting place; I'd just walk the miles until I saw his car coming, then stick out my thumb, hitching a ride. He'd zoom right past me without a glance, making me run and yell, *Hey stop!* Every week. Once back at The Farm, we'd change into our swimsuits and head to the pool. Clambering onto his back in the water, I could feel the city heat coming off his skin, feel the week pulling away. The late evening sun stretching cooler across the lawn, my dad tossing me through the air above the pool, and every Friday night, I was the happiest girl on earth.

The rest of the weekend was family regattas, outdoor games of *Pikapolka* that went on for miles, the three brothers, half-bombed, driving around on big yellow tractors (purportedly for a reason) and, once a year, on his birthday, my grandfather Pops playing "Polly Wolly Doodle" on the banjo by the pool. I remember these as idyllic times, and only learned later from my parents that trouble had begun to brew.

After Grandfather had died and the family dissolved, The Farm was sold, and finally freed of filial obligations, my father began to buy islands.

The first was in the long-pined-for lakes of northern Ontario, and purposely far from the regatta circuit. It came with an old wood cabin, big enough for just one hermit. My father raised the roof, pushed back the walls as far as beams could bear, and turned them to glass.

During the first summer after renovations were complete, he'd sit in a large armchair in the center of his house, a whiskey in one hand and a chain saw at his feet, looking out at the rocks and vast water. And every once in a while he'd get a peeved look on his face, stand up, drain his glass, pick up his chain saw, pull on his Wellingtons, and walk on down to the dock.

He'd fire up his massive inboard and roar across the bay to a neighboring island. Start up the chain saw and cut down tree after tree, selectively carving his view—readying it for transfer to canvas.

In his late forties, he quits smoking, gains thirty pounds, loses them, and tells us his recurring erotic dream: standing naked on the beach, smoking a cigarette.

Because I was a glad tomboy for the first twelve years of my life, my father treated me like a son when it came to, well, just about everything. At tennis he'd ace me right out of the game, plow me down on the squash court if I got in his way, and I was relieved when he stopped coming to matches at school, critiquing my play at halftime. It didn't occur to me until much later that he might have needed some warning before my obsession turned abruptly from horses to boys, and the dreaded first date was upon us.

I was thirteen, I guess, and he was a boy named Mark who lived down the street. We were going to the movies at seven.

Because I had only just begun to mutate from hardcore tomboy, the mainstay of my panic and dread was the idea of having to be ladylike—assisted here by my brother, who kept asking if I was sure Mark knew I wasn't a guy, and my sister freaking me out with stories of tongues and kissing and where hands may wander and grope. The afternoon hours of growing unease, spent muscling into hated, dainty outfits, then padding down the hall to the full-length mirror, and my mother's "Oh, goodness, is that what you're wearing? And remember, you mustn't smell sweaty, darling . . ." And on until 6:30 P.M.

Gentle, kind, and Clearasiled Mark arrives and we're breathless, looking mostly at our shoes (*and polish your shoes, dear; a boy notices that sort of thing*)—"hi" "hi" "heh, yeah, hi"—wiping sweaty palms on our bums, goofy kid smiles flashy with braces. Some agony later, it's "Wanna go?" and just then, my father enters the room. Mark smiles so politely and straightens his tie, offers his moist hand to shake, and lets the pater know that he works at Grand & Toy stationery two afternoons a week so, "Your daughter is in good hands." And my father, my tall and broad father with his deep rich-man voice and who knows the full tizzy I'm in, keeps hold of the gulping boy's hand and asks:

So, Mark, are you much of a boxer?
Um, sorry?
Box. Do you box? Would you care to go a couple of rounds?
. . . Sir?

Then father lets go the hand, walks into the kitchen, and brings back two pairs of oven mitts, smiling, "Gail loves to box. Hell of a swing. Come on, sweetie, let's show him what you've got." And he holds out the mitts to me, dead serious. I stare at them and stare and blush and:

What?

Now he's slipping on the second mitt, and his dukes are up.

Come on!
. . . What?

Clutching my pair of flower-patterned, heat-resistant gloves and thinking that death seemed a very viable option. Then he punches me in the shoulder.

Come on, come fill me in!

He keeps going and goading me, fancy footing and grinning around like Mohammed Ali as we're trying to get past him. And I know he's not going to stop. So I'm mad and I spin around with my fist balled saying, "Cut it out," and swing, not aiming. Then it's "Oh jeez," from my dad as he crumbles to the floor.

I'd got him right in the solar plexus, and knocked his wind out. He's on the floor, oven mitts rubbing his belly, and wheezing, "Oh, boy."

Now probably too chicken to call it off, Mark walks me to the theater not saying a thing the whole way, and he ducks all through the movie each time I reach for the popcorn. And though he's hung up his gloves and switched to slightly subtler techniques, my father has yet to approve of any man in my life. So it goes.

It was around this same time that, after years of devotion to a foreseeable lifestyle, my father began to drift more and more from his family. He took long painting trips alone in summer months, to the Arctic and Greece, and the rest of the year spent more and more time in his studio—a freezing cold room in the back of the house where he'd drink and paint and play seventies pop music long into the night. While not banned from going there, I understood that it was his private sanctum. The only time I was invited in, and the only time my father ever asked for my help or advice on anything, was just before a show when he needed to name his paintings.

He kept a running list of possible titles and, because his art at the time was geometrical abstract, just about anything could apply. On the list, among Hallmark sentiments and industrial spare parts, was *Circular plug,* which sent me and, once over the insult, my dad into fits of laughter—saying we should call them all that. Special series. Done. It became our one private and running joke, and the name we'd shout out whenever stumped by what to call a painting, though none ever earned the honor.

He tacks a white sheet over a doorway, shines it with gel-covered klieg lights, and has us dance colored shadows to the Beatles and Trashmen.

The Christmas after my parents divorced, Dad went off on a singles sailing cruise in the Caribbean and our mother came to the house to spend the holidays with the three kids. At 2 A.M. on Christmas Eve, the pipes in my father's studio burst and water began gushing out onto his paintings. Mom came to wake us up, and we grumbled downstairs to begin moving the canvases to another room.

She'd begun in a frenzy, splashing over the floor, ordering us to go quicker and quicker, then rushed out to call the fire department. But when she came back, she was suddenly spent— stood there just watching us, then broke down. Nobody says anything. We move silently back and forth past our mother, who stands soaked and weeping in the doorway, hauling landscapes through freezing water, naked pictures of Dad's lovers floating around our feet.

During long rides in the car, he waits for our favorite songs to come on the radio and starts shouting stupid lyrics overtop of them: "Light me baby, light my fire! Yeah, gimme a match now, gimme a match! Oh baby, oh baby, I'm burning now!"

He was one of those men who grew more handsome over the years, attracting scores of women with his charm and wit and, weirdly enough, the flirtation skills of a schoolboy. After the divorce, they begin to flock round. The temporarily unattached women who've made a steady career of being wealthy men's wives. They're slick and practiced, and on a first-name basis with all the town's best divorce lawyers. Their top piece of advice on the matter is, "Honey, get a Jew." They're wrapped tight in designer slut, drenched in platinum perfume, and wet whisper their willingness to do anything. They bring us food and wine and expensive gifts.

Most nights, there's a dinner party. Three or four rivals, all shimmy and creamy and high-pitched laughter. He doesn't care about any of them and can't remember their names, so he just calls them all *sweetie*. Pretty soon, he's calling us *sweetie*, too, and offering us screwdrivers for breakfast.

All the kids have moved temporarily back to the house, but it's becoming increasingly awkward to watch our father's adolescence. My brother snaps first, slips out one night, and heads to the West Coast for good. It takes Dad a week to notice he's gone. A few months later, I leave for university in a neighboring province, and the distance from my father begins to grow. Our only time together in the years that follow is a weekend spent boozing and stumbling around the Plains of Abraham in old Quebec City, commiserating on how much love stinks except when it doesn't.

Soon after, the house is sold and Dad moves temporarily to his studio in a converted warehouse he owns on the bad side of town. He's embarked on his own sixties revolution, denied him twenty years earlier, occasionally enticing bourgeois friends to come slum in the neighborhood taverns, draft beer and weak G&Ts among crackheads and dirt-poor drunks. His interest in work is waning as he paints more and more, at times helped by naked women rolling on canvas. Full expression of his freak and safe forays into dangerous territory. He's getting it out of his system.

Now into his senior citizenry, he moves back to the quiet leafy crescents of his childhood and, to everyone's surprise and relief, marries a mature, self-sufficient woman not prone to indulging his whims. Winters are spent in their lush tropical home, and the rest of the year divided between their other properties and trips to wherever they please. He has retired from architecture, and from paternal duty it seems, our only contact now a brief call at Christmas and when someone has died. We keep making plans to travel the ocean, spend some time, and agree how wonderful it would be, but never seem to get around to it.

He lines all twelve kids up in front of him, looking us each in the eye, one by one, then he begins to giggle, louder and louder till he's red with laughter, daring us to keep a straight face. We squirm, bite our tongues, trying not to give in. I usually last about thirty seconds. By the end it's just my sister and cousin Scott, going purple with trying to stay stony-faced. Then they break to the cheers of everyone laughing their heads off.

A native of Canada, Gail Armstrong is a writer and translator who lives in France. She used to write daily at openbrackets.com.

Not My Problem

Bill Farrell

The parking lot at our local grocery store has all the features we've come to know and love about parking lots. It's big and flat with up and down arrows clearly painted on the surface. There are speed bumps to deter the NASCAR drivers out for a loaf of bread and a quart of milk, and stop signs placed to be ignored.

And usually, it's devoid of drama aside from the occasional pair of blackbirds engaged in a french-fry tug-of-war.

I pushed my cart laden with groceries across the parking lot to my car as I have a thousand times before without incident, mindful of the occasional lunatic driving the wrong way, or the blind person backing out at full speed. As I loaded my purchases into the trunk of my car, my thoughts were on the barbecue planned after I returned home. Steaks on the grill with all the fixings would be a nice end to a quiet weekend.

After returning the cart to the corral, I strolled back to the car, thinking about whether to use chives or green onions in the potato salad. My thoughts were interrupted by a shout.

"Jake! Jake! No!"

Now, there are shouts and there are shouts. You hear shouts at a baseball game like, "Go Bears!" but it's more like "Go Bearrrrs!" and it's a happy, excited kind of shout full of laughter and cheer.

Then there's the kind of shout that's like a question, "Is anybody home?" The inflection rises at the end, uncertain.

And then there's the panicky shout that is short and to the point with a hint of desperation.

"Jake! Jake! No!" was a desperate, panicky shout.

I looked around to hear more shouting, "Jake! Stop, Jake!" shouting that was now Panicky with a capital "P."

As I recalled the scene with 20/20 hindsight: four-year-old Jake, sporting a maniacal grin, ran toward me between parked cars as fast as his little legs could go. In the background was his mother in pursuit.

As a bystander my first instinct was to watch the drama play out: after all, it wasn't my business. Jake and his mom had to sort this out.

Then I heard the telltale call of the yahoo, that is, the throaty vroom of a big-engined pickup truck driven by a small-brained teenager. Typically, the yahoo's last words are "Hey, y'all, watch this!" I looked around and confirmed my suspicions. Roaring across the parking lot, leaping over speed bumps as only a big-wheeled pickup truck can do, came a black Ford sporting roof lights and a large chromed grille suitable for a locomotive.

It didn't take a degree in mathematics to calculate that Jake was heading into the path of this monster truck from between the parked cars. The driver would not be able to see Jake in time to stop but, in any case, at the speed the truck was going, it wouldn't matter.

It could be that Jake saw the truck and was running to get a closer look. It could be that Jake was about to trip and fall over. It could be that the truck driver was about to stop and park his truck. It could be there were other possibilities that would have played out.

But what happened was this. I bent down and scooped up Jake by his armpits and held him there at eye level. In that split second Jake and I regarded each other. Jake's red hair stuck out at all angles. He grasped a partially melted chocolate bar, much of which was on his face blending in nicely with his freckles. He struggled a little, wiping melted chocolate on my sleeve and on the side of my face. I held him tightly, nevertheless.

"Where you going, little feller?" I asked.

The monster truck drove by; Jake followed it with his eyes.

"Twuk," Jake said, and pointed with his chocolate bar.

"Yes," I said, "big twuk. Where's your mommy?"

Jake turned his head around just as his mother, wide-eyed and out of breath, reached us.

"Mommy!" Jake struggled in my hands. I changed my grip so I could hand him over to his mother.

She held him close for a moment then unleashed a short burst of Mother's Fury.

"Jake, you stop when I say stop, you hear? You could get yourself squashed flat running around in a parking lot."

Jake stuck his candy bar in his mouth and was quiet.

Jake's mom looked at me briefly and said, "Thanks. Sorry for the trouble," and turned to walk back to their car. Jake, in tow, was getting a second lecture.

Released from duty, I drove home.

On the way I reflected on the small drama that had unfolded in the parking lot. Looking back at a time before I had kids of my own, I saw myself standing back, letting little Jake scamper to his destiny. Not my problem.

I saw myself looking at a sticky, chocolate-covered, undisciplined child, out of control and standing back. Not my problem.

I saw myself just getting into my own car and driving home to fix barbecue dinner, maybe reading about the young Jake tragedy in the newspaper the next day.

"Not my problem" would have been a time before I had kids of my own, before I became a father.

Once I became a father, I accepted a responsibility for all children, not just my own. It came with the job. I committed to an obligation to serve and protect all children.

They should issue badges when you become a father.

So, as a father I couldn't stand by and allow little Jake to run to his destiny. He could do that another time.

Later that evening, relating to my wife my great adventure at the grocery store, she commented, "I remember a time when you wouldn't pick up a clean kid you knew. And you just reached down and picked up a strange kid? Boy, have you changed."

Yes, I had changed, but when did it happen? Little did I know how long it would take to answer that question.

The Manual

"What do you think about kids?" my wife asked.

"They're okay," I replied.

That was the only time we talked about kids, to my recollection. Maybe all those other conversations have been obliterated by cosmic rays or something, but that's the one I remember.

We were walking to our home in London from the pub. Our spirits were high, as we had downed a couple of pints of London Pride, a highly spirited ale.

Married only a few months, we had not really discussed kids. We were both students working to finish our degrees, looking for that first job. The prospect of settling down and having a bunch of kids was far, far out on the horizon.

Yes, far, far away. Way, way out there. An infinite, cosmic expanse of time.

Four years, to be exact.

Walking into the delivery room at 6 o'clock in the morning was a far cry from that gentle evening's stroll home not so many years ago. Circumstances had changed considerably. Totally out of character, my wife had urged me to run red lights.

"Hospital," she'd gasped, "now. Don't stop. Don't stop!" It was the gasping and instructions that got us into this situation in the first place, but instinct told me now was not the time to address fine historical points. Just drive.

The delivery room operated in two completely different space-time continuums: a speedy, fast get-things-done-now time for us, and a slow-motion, laid-back, whatever time for the medical staff. While I flitted from bed to door to monitoring equipment to bed to door, the doctors and nurses moved with sloth-like slowness, very deliberately and with no concern.

"Are you trained?"

I stopped in my tracks and turned to the nurse who had asked the question.

"Trained? No, I'm not a doctor, that is, not a medical doctor—I'm a chemist but I don't do much chemistry and I work with computers and—" I babbled, but the nurse cut me short.

"Have you and your wife taken childbirth classes?" she asked.

I looked into her eyes, which showed the patience of a thousand births, and said, "Yes, but we haven't finished the course."

She smiled and said, "You'll finish the course this morning. You have work to do. Here's a damp cloth and some ice chips."

Wow, it was just like the film. I began to apply what I had learned and shortly became a world-class expert in Brow Wiping and Ice Chip Delivering.

I was surprised by how fast it all ended. Suddenly, the doctor appeared, there was a flurry of activity, and through the ruckus I heard someone say, "Nice catch!" and "It's a little girl."

I was a father.

I had a daughter and I knew her name only because we had decided on names the night before. I heard the nurses calling out the numbers and statistics, and I knew what they meant because I had studied for months. I was prepared for the name and the numbers, but I was not prepared for the nurse and the baby.

"Here's your daughter."

"What? Oh, uh, maybe you should give her to my wife. She's the baby person. Over there. I'll hold her later, heh, heh, okay?"

The nurse fixed me with a gaze that would have defeated Alexander.

"Sit down now so you can hold your daughter. I'll show you how," she said gently, unblinking.

I sat in the chair and the nurse handed me my daughter, instructing me to hold her body here and support her head there.

I was as rigid as a statue. Looking back, I think it was the first time in my entire life I had held a live baby. Not the doll or sack of flour like we used in the class, but a real baby—a real person. I tried to smile and look nonchalant, but I was relieved when the nurse told me my time was up and we had to go.

Over the next few days I got a chance to hold my daughter a few times and we fell into a routine in the hospital. Feeding, cleaning, visiting, and back to the nursery. Life was grand.

When it came time for us to go home, there was great fanfare in the ward. We were given a ceremonious wheelchair ride to the front door; presented a cart of balloons, flowers, and supplies; packed into our car; and sent on our way.

Our house was quiet. I unpacked all the stuff and Helen took our daughter to her room for a feeding and a nap.

That's when it hit me like a brick wrapped in a diaper, like a face-full of strained prunes, like a cry at 2 A.M. What do I do now?

I couldn't believe that the hospital let us take a baby home and we don't even have a manual. How could they be so irresponsible? All the classes we took taught us how to get us to this point, but what do we do now?

Not only had I never changed a real diaper on a real baby, but where was I going to find a baseball glove for hands that small? I had more questions than answers.

Little did I know, that would never change.

There is something to be said for the phrase "day by day." Just take it one day at a time, they say. Each day was a new adventure and we were amazed at how excited we were about little changes. Sitting up was a big deal. Crawling gave us personal entertainment. Walking was a milestone and speaking drew us into rapt attention.

In time the manual wrote itself. What they never told you is that your child will write the manual, adding a few words every day.

As a father, my job was to support the author, edit the work when I could, and hope that the book would be a best seller.

Driving Me Dizzy

I have never been obsessed with the color of a vehicle. Sure, I wouldn't be too keen to drive something lime green or hot pink, but when you buy a car, you can't always get what you want. But if you try sometimes, you'll get what you need.

I drove up the driveway, parked the car, and beeped the horn a few times. The kids came out to see what the ruckus was about, but the ruckus had not yet begun.

"What's this?" my daughter asked, wrinkling up her nose as if she were staring at a dead rat on wheels.

"It's our new car," I said brightly. "Cool, huh?"

Daughter's face expressed a frozen mask of horror. The blood drained from her cheeks. Her voice quivered.

"It's gray," she whispered hoarsely, "gray. You bought a gray car?"

Her voice rising, she turned and looked at me in utter amazement as if I had a geranium growing out of my forehead and demanded in a shrill voice, "You bought a gray car?"

And before I could educate her that the car wasn't exactly gray, rather the hue was called "Pacific Mist," she screamed hysterically, "How could you do this to me? You have ruined my life!"

She said something else I didn't catch as she turned, ran upstairs, and slammed the door to her room.

I looked at the gray car in the driveway, convincing myself that it really was Pacific Mist. Maybe Pacific Mist at night, or Pacific Mist in fog, or optimistically, Pacific Mist on a partly cloudy day.

Aw, face it, it was gray; the last car on the lot, and even under a bright light, like a supernova, it looked Pacific-Mist-ish.

At breakfast the following morning my daughter, who was learning to drive at the time, informed me that she would never drive the "gray" car. She'd rather walk, or if forced, she'd drive the van.

I tried a subtle marketing strategy.

"You'd drive the van?" I asked. "It's purple. You call it Grape-O. Are you telling me you'd drive old Grape-O rather than the new car, Pacific Mist?"

The strategy failed.

My daughter looked at me as if I were a man from Mars.

"Well, duh," she snorted, "I'd ride a mule to school before I'd drive the gray loser mobile."

There was a "beep" outside and Daughter grabbed her backpack, ran out the front door, and into the open door of her classmate's red BMW. With a roar, they disappeared down the street and around the corner.

I poured myself a cup of coffee and thought about my mistake of buying a Pacific Mist car rather than a red BMW. The issue wasn't so much the color of the car as it was a shock to my daughter's expectations. If I had driven home the same car but painted Volcano Red, I would have been a hero. I was the goat. A gray goat. I guess I could have taken the time to include her in the decision, but that thought only reminded me of her reaction a few weeks ago.

"Hey, I'm going out to look at new cars. Want to come along?"

Observing me curiously as if examining an insect under a magnifying glass, my daughter sighed and tried her best to educate me.

"Let me get this straight," she started pedantically. "Go with you to a hot, smelly car place where a salesman with greasy hair will stare at my butt the whole time, or go shopping at the mall with my friends and hang out with cool people."

She paused for maximum effect then said, "I'll go with Cool People for 500, Dad. Say 'hi' to Click and Clack for me, or is it Clack and Click?"

I poured another cup of coffee and reflected on the time we went to the city dump a few years ago. We had some old furniture to get rid of and scraps of this and that, and I figured I could pile it all into Grape-O and make one trip to the city dump. I asked my daughter if she wanted to go along and she leapt at the idea like a duck on a june bug.

We loaded up the van and drove out to the dump. We sang "Hundred Bottles of Beer on the Wall," stopped to watch a farmer plowing a field, and laughed as we bounced along the gravel road to the dump. At the dump we watched seagulls wheel around in the sky, climbed on the giant bulldozer, and talked to the superintendent, who had a very big, friendly, slobbery dog. It was a great trip on a Saturday afternoon and one that my daughter would talk about for years.

But then things changed. One day my daughter was emptying the dishwasher and, holding up a coffee cup, asked, "Where does this go?"

"The same place it has gone for the past ten years," I replied, "on the coffee cup shelf."

"Where's that?"

"Right in front of you where you put the coffee cups last week."

She slammed the coffee cup on the counter, startling the cats and causing me to look up in alarm.

Red-faced, she spluttered, "Well, if you're going to keep moving things around, how can you expect me to do anything around here?" Her chest heaved, her eyes wild. She ran upstairs to her bedroom and slammed the door.

"What's up with that?" I asked Cat, who was the only other person in the kitchen.

Cat blinked at me and proceeded to lick his tail.

"I thought so," I said.

As a father, you have to learn to be absolutely, rigidly flexible. I call it the ARF principle. Absolutely means you will always be there. Rigidly means you will weather any storm, any tantrum, and any irrationality. Flexible means that everything is subject to change without notice, don't try this at home, your mileage may vary, batteries not included, one part will be missing, and this page intentionally left blank.

As a father you have to learn to be absolutely, rigidly flexible. I call it the ARF principle. Absolutely means you will always be there. Rigidly means you will weather any storm, any tantrum, and any irrationality. Flexible means that everything is subject to change without notice, don't try this at home, your mileage may vary, batteries not included, one part will be missing, and this page intentionally left blank.

Some weeks later came the final catastrophe—Grape-O was in the shop and Daughter needed a car.

"You'll have to take the gray car, I mean, Pacific Mist. Here are the keys."

I handed my daughter the keys. Reluctantly, she drove off in the gray car that had ruined her life.

Hours later she returned humming to herself, walked up to me, and gave me a hug.

"What's that all about?" I asked, quite surprised by the reception.

"The gray car is really cool," she said, "All my friends really like it and it's so zippy and has a great sound system. You never told me how much fun it is to drive. I think you just wanted to drive it all by yourself. But I forgive you. Can I have my own key? Thanks!"

Without waiting for an answer, she ran upstairs to spend a few months on the phone. I opened the kitchen junk drawer, rummaged around for a key ring, and fixed a key to it.

"I wonder if she'll remember where the coffee cups go," I asked Cat.

Cat blinked.

Conversations with a Cat

Kink hopped into my lap, looked at me momentarily, then settled in between my left leg and the arm of the chair. My laptop was perched precariously on my right leg. It was like sitting under two hot-water bottles and in just a few minutes sweat was running down my leg.

"One of you has got to go," I said. So, I closed the lid to my laptop and placed it on the end table. Recognizing the available real estate, Kink stretched out and offered his head for a scratch.

Aside from Kink's purring, the house was quiet.

"Where is everybody?" I asked Kink.

Kink looked up and stated the obvious. "They've all moved away."

"Whew," I said, "that was fast. Somehow I thought it would last forever. Sometimes it seemed so."

"Don't ask me," scolded Kink, "I wasn't here. My life is short enough as it is without you getting all dark on me."

"You look pretty healthy to me," I noted.

"You're happy with the Shreddy Chicken, Kat Chow Bits, and Catnip Snax," I added, "and the occasional table treat and bowl of milk. You'd prefer clawing trash bags on the street instead?"

Kink looked up, yawned, stretched to his full length, and hooked his claws into my spare tire to get my attention. He had me from "Meow."

"Don't get me wrong," Kink continued, "you've got the care thing down pat. It took you all your life to get to this point. My point is that I'm surprised that you're surprised."

"How so?" I asked.

"Well, I moved in a few months ago when I was a kitten. I didn't come with a manual. How did you know what to do? How did you know when I was hungry, or thirsty, or wanted to play, or needed to sleep?"

"I don't know, exactly," I mused, "I guess I watched you and tried different foods until I discovered you went nuts for Shreddy Chicken. And I played with you until you collapsed into sleep, then I'd put you on the soft chair by the window as you napped. I guess I played it by ear."

Kink hopped off my lap, walked to the front door, and sat on the mat regarding the mockingbirds playing outside.

After a few minutes Kink turned, regarded me carefully, and said, "They had to go, you know. Just as I chase mockingbirds in my dreams, they had to go out to chase their own dreams. Your job was to prepare them. How'd you do?"

Well, that's the $64,000 Question.

Door Number 2.

I'll take "Success in Life for 500," Alex.

"I don't know, Kink," I said, "the story's not over. I worked on the plot, tried to develop the characters, and used as many action verbs as I could, but I just don't know how it ends."

"You can't know how it ends," Kink demurred. "You can do your best and no more than that. Nobody requires more than that."

Do your best, I thought. Simple, but how do you know what your best could be? What you think is your best is not what someone else might think is your best. The fishing lesson was a good example.

As my daughter grew into her teens, it came to me one fitful night that I had never taken her fishing. Not exactly true— we went to a few picnics where fishing poles were available for the kids to use, but we had never had that special father-daughter bonding experience that could only be had by fishing together, just the two of us.

Remorse set in and in a few weeks I was consumed with a need bordering on obsession to go fishing with my daughter. Fortunately, I had a friend who was an avid fisherman and he agreed to take us out on the Gulf for a fishing trip.

Thus it was on the way home from soccer practice that I raised the subject of fishing with my daughter.

"Forgive me, Father, for I have sinned. I never took my daughter fishing and I deprived her of that special father-daughter experience and for that I am truly sorry."

I broached the subject smoothly.

"Hey, that was a great soccer practice. By the way I have a friend who will take us out on his boat to fish in the Gulf. He pretty much guarantees that you'll catch a big red snapper."

My daughter turned to look at me and said, "Fishing? You mean with hooks and bait and stuff?"

"Yeah," I said enthusiastically, "just you and me and a boat crew on the Gulf and we can fish and cut bait and hang out in the sun all day. It will be great."

"Dad," she intoned, "you have never taken me fishing. Not once. Only at picnics."

"I know," I said hanging my head, "I thought it was something we had never done and that, well, you know, a childhood thing, father, daughter . . ." I was rambling.

"You mean I don't have to go if I don't want to?" she said brightly. "This is just some sort of guilt thing?"

Children are so perceptive.

"Fishing is gross," she announced. "I'm glad you never took me fishing. I don't want to fish unless I'm on a desert island or something. If it's all the same to you, you go fish and I'll go to the mall with my friends."

I couldn't believe it. I was off the hook!

In my imagination I had committed a mortal sin, but in reality I did the right thing. By accident. How could that be?

Kink stretched out and scratched the rug, licked his flank, and wiped his left ear with his paw. Then he looked at me.

"Just as you learned how I love Catnip Snax, you learned that your kids had their own likes and dislikes. You raised them to be individual people and that's what they are. In your life, fishing was important, but in their life it isn't. You can't live your life again through your children just as you can't live your life through me. Unless, of course, you secretly crave chasing mockingbirds."

I got up out of the chair, walked over to the carpet, knelt down, and gave Kink a scratch behind the ears. Kink purred.

"I thought I could stop the clock," I told Kink, "you know, stop time. Just for a while. But I never could. The clock just went faster and faster. And like a clock, I got wound up in their activities, and before I knew it, they were all gone and I was here with you. How did that happen? How could I let that happen?"

"You couldn't stop it if you tried," Kink said. "As a father, you're the best at what you do when you're at the end of what you do. You supported, you cheered, you sympathized, you sacrificed, you learned, you laughed and cried, often at the same time, and most of all you prepared your children for this moment at which you are here with me."

Kink and I sat there on the rug. The sun had come around to the other side of the house and afternoon shadows played across the floor.

"How'd I do?" I asked Kink.

Kink sat straight like one of those Egyptian cat statues. He gazed out the window unblinking for several minutes. The red, setting sun reflected in Kink's eyes.

Kink turned, walked to where I was sitting on the rug, climbed into my lap, and settled down. When he was comfortable, he looked up at me and said:

"You did your best."

Kink and I sat there, silently, as the sun dipped below the horizon and night fell.

∽

Bill Farrell is a writer living in Texas, having retired from a major oil company after twenty-six years of supporting computer systems, programming, and developing Web sites. Legend has it that Bill helped Al Gore create the Internet. A former class clown, Bill managed, nevertheless, to survive raising three children. Bill devotes his time and cooking prowess to supporting the Boy Scouts in a number of Scoutmaster and staff positions including international assignments. In his spare time, and let's face it, that's all his time, Bill reviews recipes for cookbooks and is an avid supporter of science education. Bill resides in Sugar Land, Texas, with his wife, Helen, and their cats, Sandy and Kink. His blog is 12tutufondue.blogspot.com.